GHOSTS OF THE SOUTH EAST

GHOSTS

OF THE SOUTH EAST

Andrew Green

Originally published by David & Charles
Reprint published 1981 by Rochester Press
ISBN 0 905540 73 5
Printed by Whitstable Litho Ltd.,
Whitstable Kent

CONTENTS

ACKNOWLEDGEMENTS

To all those kind people who helped me compile this collection through carrying out searches in various records, spending valuable time discussing details of hauntings in their own or other homes and lending me their personal notes may I offer my sincere thanks.

In particular I would like to acknowledge the assistance provided by Vera Akers of Willesborough, Jenni Balow of *Kent Messenger*, Major T. D. Bevan of Shorncliffe, Bill Buckman of Cheriton, Anne Burnaby of Mountfield, Patricia Corney of Ticehurst, Phyllis Fretwell of Steyning, Dick Godden of Folkestone, Madge Harmer of Ticehurst, Frank Hennig of *Radio Brighton*, Mrs P. Knowlden of Boxley, Mr and Mrs Le May of Pashley Manor, Marilyn Pearson of Maidstone, Charles Pizzey and Eddie Pratt of Caterham, Sheila Simmons of Hollingbourne and Ron Woodgate of Robertsbridge. I am indebted to Rev Canon Greville Cooke for so kindly allowing me to use lines from his sonnet on Michelham Priory, Molly Pears for permitting me to use extracts from her booklet *Michelham Priory*, and Commander Harrison of the Sussex Archaeological Society for his valued assistance.

But my deepest and heartfelt thanks go to my niece Deirdre Borner of Whyteleafe for typing, correcting and providing valuable comments and suggestions and to my great friend Marian Williams of Robertsbridge for the considerable help, encouragement and assistance in producing this book.

PREFACE

The South East region could justifiably claim to be the most ghost-ridden area of Great Britain, containing as it does the famous haunted village of Pluckley in Kent, the renowned Loseley Park in Surrey and the phantoms of Brede Place in Sussex. Some hauntings are greatly publicised and others remain known only to a few.

What I have tried to do in this selection is to offer a representative collection of ghosts of the three counties but to treat the stories in a way which will, I hope, prove popular among readers not greatly concerned about strict authenticity. Some phantoms can be positively identified, others like those at Eyhorne and Pashley remain unknown so in those cases I offer what could be possible answers in a fashion which may not appeal to the more serious investigator.

The majority of readers, however, will, I trust, enjoy the result.

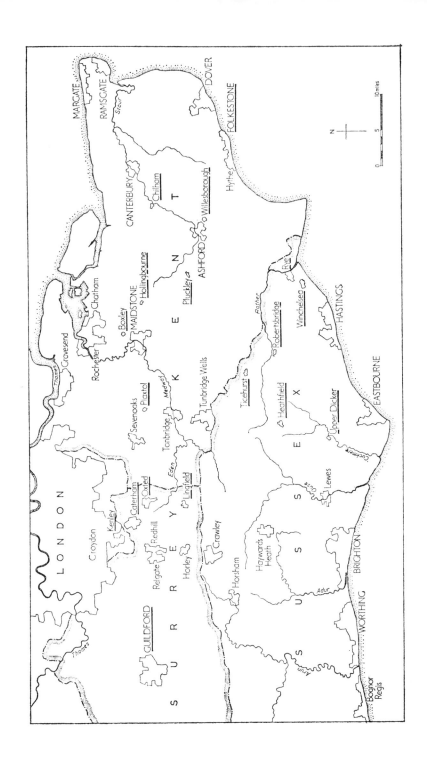

CHAPTER 1

EYHORNE MANOR, HOLLINGBOURNE

Romantic legend and myth encompass most rural areas, and in the countryside surrounding England's most haunted village of Pluckley, numerous intriguing tales are heard. The memory of a pair of twelfth-century Siamese twins, the Biddenden Maids, is perpetuated in the special cakes distributed locally on Easter Monday, the round-topped windows, known as 'Dering' windows, fitted to the majority of houses in Pluckley remind folk of the escape of a Royalist from Lady Dering's manor house and the handsome effigy of Lady Culpeper in Hollingbourne Church recalls the troubled days of royal intrigue and Civil War.

Hollingbourne, ignored by the majority of touring motorists for it lies off the main Maidstone trunk road, has been called a village of mystery yet forms a quiet community of differing stratas, all linked by an atmosphere of history and charm.

One expert claims the name derived from the abundance of holly trees on the surrounding hillside which act as a backcloth to the bourne which runs through the hamlet. Others state that it was originally known as Holybrook because the stream or bourne leads to the legendary site of an abbey at Leeds a few miles away.

Mention of the community certainly appears in records of AD 980 when 'Hollingburn' was granted by Athelstan, son of King Ethelred, to the church of Canterbury and in 1015 this gift was confirmed.

Many reminders of some of the olden days are happily

retained and include Godfrey House built in 1587, the Elizabethan manor house, Tanyard House and of course the old church.

This ancient building sited nearly a mile from the main sector of the village creates the focal point of another community. It was in the doorway of this old structure that a lady who lived next door saw the phantom of a man wearing green knee breeches and clothing of the Regency period.

In the 1930s Lime Kiln Cottages were affected by poltergeist activity which included the throwing of cucumbers around the kitchen, but like all such phenomena the trouble eventually ceased and is now nearly forgotten by the locals. What is not forgotten, nor ever will be, is that Greenway Court once housed the Culpeper family and it is believed that the manor house was also closely associated with the same famous name. It was in one of these properties that many years were spent by the four daughters embroidering and lace-making, primarily for the benefit of the church, but also no doubt for friends and relatives.

The memorial to their mother, Lady Elizabeth, in the Culpeper Chapel shows her wearing some of the exquisite lace as an example of her daughters' renowned craft and expertise with the needle. Her husband, Sir Thomas, was a Royalist and when he joined King Charles in exile for some twelve years the girls continued to work in England producing a beautiful length of fine cloth which they hoped would eventually form the altar decoration when the troubled days were over. The material is still in existence but no longer on display.

The southern outskirts of the main village were termed in Anglo-Saxon times as Eyhorne Street being derived from *ey*, water and *horn*, a turning or bend, but if one stands now in the front doorway of Eyhorne Manor it is difficult to visualise that it orginally formed the corner of the village green during the fifteenth century. Unfortunately, little is known of its early history except that it was probably built in about 1410 as a yeoman's hall house, being a typical Wealden building with a central hall and fireplace in the centre of the living area.

The building is timber-framed with the usual overhanging gables and contains a rare smoking bay which can be examined by the many visitors who are justifiably attracted to the house, for it is open to the public on Saturday and Sunday afternoons in the summer.

Many reminders of former occupants have been found in the manor over the years, but more especially during the twenty years of renovation carried out unaided by the current owners, Derek and Sheila Simmons. Three marbles were discovered in the ashes of the original fire, a child's shoe was found propped against the firestack in the loft and a French water bottle was taken from the floor of what is now the dining-room. Demanding even greater attention is the medieval terracotta seal found in the foundations, for it portrays a man and woman on horseback in front of a large building, possibly Leeds Castle or Abbey.

During my very enjoyable visit, I was able to add further relics of a bygone era, that of a tusk and tooth of a wild boar which joined the cluster of oyster shells which had presumably been thrown out of the dining-room window some three-hundred and fifty years ago.

One of the most attractive features of the unique site is the overall charm created by the concentration of fragrant herbs, not just in bowls in every room or hanging from the walls but crowding every flower bed in the beautiful cottage garden.

When the Simmonses bought Eyhorne Manor it comprised three small, rather dilapidated cottages and a former occupant of one of them was able to recall the weird phenomena which she and her children experienced there between the spring of 1941 and the autumn of 1950.

Both her daughter Sally and young son Alan were frequently frightened by 'someone walking up the stairs' and although

11

Mrs Brunger herself had often heard the heavy tread of an invisible phantom she had made courageous attempts to convince the family that the noise was due to 'anything else I could think of at that moment. The wind, perhaps, or even mice. But I couldn't convince myself, let alone the kids'.

Sally, when she was four years old, occupied the little back room at the top of the house and one evening just before going upstairs to bed asked her mother if she thought she would see the little old lady that night. 'It gave me quite a creepy feeling to realise that she had seen what later became known as "the lady in grey"'. It seems that she would often listen to the old woman telling her stories, but her voice was in such a low whisper that Sally could hear only indistinctly.

Mrs Brunger would often creep past the bedroom door to hear her daughter quietly chatting to the old lady who, according to Sally, was always standing in a corner of the room at the foot of the bed. When the family moved the young girl was quite upset and said that she would miss her nightly visitor.

'But what was the most scaring thing about the place was the slithering, like silk or taffeta, that I could hear in Sally's bedroom when it was empty and the cold clammy feeling in the corner of the room by the bed.'

Not only was the house affected for, when gardening one afternoon, Mrs Brunger looked up to see the figure of a little man in a black suit watching her from the corner of the plot. She greeted the stranger but, receiving no reply, returned to her work only to look back a couple of seconds later to see that the man had gone. 'But there was nowhere for him to go except into my cottage and he hadn't gone in there. At one time a small black dog would visit us and he would sometimes stop in a particular spot of the garden and growl with all his hackles raised. There was nothing there, but he would be looking at the spot where the little man had stood.'

Several smaller incidents which occurred during Mrs Brunger's stay convinced her and the neighbours that Eyhorne Manor really was haunted. One of the most peculiar events was when a clothes peg lifted off the washing-line, fell to the ground and vanished. It was never found again.

Confirming the belief of the existence of an unknown phantom was the report that the gentleman living in the other end of the building had seen the figure of a lady in grey moving down a corridor.

A builder had purchased all three cottages in the 1950s but because of a clash of personality between him and the house he sold it to the Simmons family. There was always the feeling of an unseen presence in the front bedroom and one of his sons, when very young, saw a man's face at the window.

Another witness to the continuing phenomena was the husband of one of the tenants who had enquired of his wife as to the identity of the little man in the green velvet suit who had come into the dining-room when his wife was cleaning brasses in the kitchen. No one else had seen the figure and he was never seen, or at least reported, again.

Mr Moon, a carpenter and builder by trade, has a keen interest in many activities but especially history and old buildings. He pointed out one of the interesting things about Eyhorne is that most of the house is made of witch elm. 'English elm is a knotty wood with character and is an attractive material, but witch elm with its straight unblemished lines is a bit weird.' Does wood create its own atmosphere one wonders, especially a timber that is associated with witch-craft?

'The whole area round here has its peculiar stories. A ghostly horseman has been seen riding the Pilgrim's Way in the evenings and quite recently the phantom girl of Bluebell Hill has been reported again', he continued. This is an often-quoted tale of motorists picking up an attractive teenager hitch-hiking on the road just outside Maidstone, and when asked to take her to her parents' home arrive to be told by the elderly couple that the girl was killed in a car crash years before. The mystified driver returns to his car to find the girl has vanished.

Sheila Simmons, who had lived in the Maidstone district for seven years, moved into Eyhorne Manor with her husband in 1952 and immediately noticed the cold, uncanny feeling of the house. Her mother-in-law occupied the end rooms whilst the Simmonses took over the other two cottages and began to carry out the massive renovation.

Almost at once Sheila heard the slithering noises in the far corner of the affected bedroom. 'It was not very nice', she told me, 'when standing in the empty room to suddenly hear a sound as if silk was being pulled along the floor towards you. Actually I was petrified and on one occasion I was so scared I just ran out of the house into the garden to get away from the thing'. Adding to the initial fright in the bedroom was the alarm of hearing footsteps ascending the old stairway, 'always at night'.

Another incident that the new owner found puzzling was when in the sitting-room in the middle of the house, she heard a lot of people's voices coming from next door. On enquiring from a neighbour as to who might be causing the noises, she was told in a puzzled tone that the building was empty. It was weeks later that Mrs Simmons senior took possession of the end cottage.

Work progressed on restoring the old house yet still the unaccountable incidents continued.

One autumn a macintosh, hung on a peg behind the kitchen door, lifted itself into the air about two feet and fell to the floor, a spoon rose inexplicably from a table and dropped with a clatter to the boards, a metal rod across the front of the firegrate rose and fell without being touched. Sounds of chinking were heard in the bedroom 'like someone playing with small silver coins'.

There are not only human phantoms at Eyhorne for, during

one afternoon in 1960, a transparent 'chow-like dog' walked straight through a closed door.

One summer afternoon Mrs Simmons having used a pair of scissors put them on a table beside her. A few moments later they had gone. The floor was examined, the seat, the furniture, the complete room, but the scissors had completely vanished. Days later when Sheila was gardening she was astounded to find them lying in the middle of the lawn, yet clean and free from rust. Weeks later the performance was repeated except that the scissors made their reappearance in the middle of the settee.

Another more frightening episode occurred in the hall which at the time was filled with rubble from the renovation work. The front door was locked and the only entrance to the room, an internal door, was closed with a large radiogram pushed hard against it. There was no possible means of access to the room but suddenly the silence of the house was broken by two loud and distinct knocks at the internal door. Sheila, quietly working in the empty room, was 'shattered'. No reason was ever found for these mysterious knocks made so purposefully by the unknown and unseen entity of Eyhorne.

At the rear of the property and acting as a border to some of the flowering herb beds, large flagstones perfectly match the setting of a typical cottage garden, but many years ago the path was formed of cinders. One morning in 1972 Sheila Simmons, having seen her husband Derek off to work, was sitting in the dining-room when she heard footsteps running round the end of the cottage and presumed her husband had returned having forgotten something he needed at the office. But the footsteps ceased and there was no one to be seen. The problem was not just the identity of the invisible person who never even reached the back door, but why were the footsteps crunching as if on pebbles—or was it cinders?

Who could it be that creeps about the front corner bedroom dragging silk or taffeta with her? Is it the same entity who idly plays with a few silver groats, pondering on whether she has been paid enough for her work? Who was it that temporarily 'borrowed' Sheila's scissors? Who hid the clothes peg?

In the 1600s a lot of the inhabitants of a tiny community such as that of Hollingbourne would be employed as servants at the manor house. The majority of the internal staff would have their own accommodation in the servants' quarters, but other artisans such as gardeners, farm workers and dress makers would return to their homes after their daily toil.

Silk and taffeta have always been expensive materials and were certainly not normally used by village peasants, so who other than nobility could have afforded such luxuries? It would be obtainable by a dressmaker who would work at home after discussing styles and measurements with her client, the lady of the manor. Is it coincidence that Mrs Simmons's specialised museum contains the equipment of a laundry, but more intriguingly, a large collection of smoothing irons of all types? Or is it that the atmosphere created by a maker of ladies' gowns has affected the interests of the current owner 400 years later? Could it be that we have perhaps identified the mysterious lady in grey, the woman who, though now unseen, continues to be heard at Eyhorne?

If we refer to old records and history books we find that Katharine Howard, future consort of Henry VIII, was reared in the nursery of her uncle, Sir John Culpeper, as a companion for his heir and Katharine's first cousin Thomas Culpeper. Fate had brought the probable lovers together very early in their lives.

But Katharine's time in Hollingbourne was short for, before reaching maturity, she was received into the family of the dowager Duchess of Norfolk where vigilance and supervision was sadly lacking. The young girl's upbringing was badly neglected and she was compelled to sleep in a dormitory with servant women whose habits and worldly knowledge had an unfortunate effect. Before even in her teens she had become 'the object of illicit passion to a low born villain in the household named Henry Manox'.

In 1533 the foster mother, the Duchess of Norfolk, took young Katharine to Lambeth probably to attend the coronaation of her granddaughter Ann Boleyn, and in the same year that Lady Howard died, a Mary Lassells was taken into the household. At that time Katharine was probably about twelve years old but possibilities of her future with Manox were already being discussed by Mary and another associate, Dorothy Barwike. The young man had made his intentions obvious by admitting that his 'designs were of a dishonourable nature and from the liberties the young lady had allowed, he had no doubt of being able to effect his purpose'. Katharine was justifiably annoyed when she heard of this and Manox apologised, but the tale was not forgotten.

Among the band of gentlemen which the Duke of Norfolk retained in his service was a Francis Derham who, although considered to be more courageous than moral, aimed at courting and winning young Katharine. Impoverished by the Duchess, but having a passion for fine silks and jewellery, she got Derham to provide many little brooches and similar ornaments for her dresses and because of her incessant craving for satins and velvets Katharine was at one time in considerable debt to Derham. However, the situation developed and love tokens were exchanged.

Having accepted so many presents from Derham and rather overwhelmed by his attentions, the future queen forgot that she was hardly the mate for a mere gentleman-at-arms and finally consented to being accepted as his fiancée. In those days this was a binding contract for marriage and Derham began to call her 'his wife' and Katharine to refer to him as 'her husband'. During her trial later she admitted that Francis sometimes 'hath come early in the morning' to her bedroom 'and much misbehaved himself but never by my request or consent'.

It was some time before the so-called guardian of Katharine, the old Duchess of Norfolk, realised to what extent the couple's affections had developed, but one day she found them 'romping together' and being greatly offended beat them both. Derham, realising that he might face death for his audacity, fled to Ireland and became a pirate for a short time.

During the absence of Francis, Katharine acquired a grace and feminine reserve and when Derham finally found means to return, secretly hoping to resume his relationship, he was highly aggrieved at being rebuffed, and more especially when hearing the report which was circulating at the time that his 'wife' was contemplating marriage to her maternal kinsman Thomas Culpeper.

Thomas had been appointed to the household of Anne of Cleves and was described by the historian Pollino as 'a most beautiful youth'. Derham, realising that his absence had lost him the chance of gaining Katharine as his legal wife, returned to Ireland even though the precocious girl claimed that she had not heard of the rumour concerning her former playmate. By the time of Katharine's removal to the Court in preparation for her regal marriage, Derham had completely vanished from the scene, but he was to return again eventually to his death.

It is believed that Henry's first encounter with his future wife was at a banquet given by Gardiner, Bishop of Winchester, a few weeks after the King's marriage to Anne. Noting the impression made by 'the very young' girl he organised further opportunities for their meeting. It should not be forgotten that the Church had expressed great horror at Henry's insistence on his marriage to 'the lady of Cleves' and the Bishop, presumably knowing how fickle the monarch was, had hoped that the situation could be amended.

One of the mysteries of English history is that, although there was a public announcement of the dissolution of Henry's marriage to Anne, there are no particulars of the solemnisation of the wedding to Katharine. It is only known that on 8 August 1540 Katharine was introduced by Henry at Hampton Court as his queen.

Perhaps because of her new status—it was, after all, enough

to occupy the throne—Katharine lost her inclination to bedeck herself in costly robes and jewellery, but she evidenced the height of foolishness and sealed her own doom by admitting her former lover, Francis Derham, into the household as a gentleman-in-waiting and private secretary.

On 29 August Thomas Culpeper had a long private interview in the Queen's privy chamber at 11 o'clock at night with only Lady Rochford being present. After many hours he departed with a chain and a rich cap and later this meeting was construed as proof of criminal intimacy.

But Culpeper was one of the gentleman of the King's privy chamber: he had been appointed at the marriage of Anne of Cleves. The real reason for his meeting with Katharine could then have been because of personal trouble at home in Hollingbourne. He had been accused of a 'frightful crime' in the village and when resisting arrest had wilfully murdered one of the sheriff's men. For some unknown reason he had been pardoned by Henry.

But early in October 1541 Archbishop Cranmer, at a select meeting of the privy council, told his colleagues details of the Queen's misconduct.

Although Thomas and Katharine had been very close companions in childhood, the 'engagement' as suspected by the forsaken and jealous lover Derham can never be proved. Sir Ralph Sadler, however, in view of mounting comment, obviously false statements and innuendo, commanded the archbishop to question the Queen again with respect to her intimacy with Culpeper. Katharine continued to deny that there had been the slightest impropriety between herself and her cousin.

Early in November Katharine was removed as a degraded prisoner from Hampton Court to Syon House, her disgrace was proclaimed and the household discharged. On 31 November Culpeper and Derham were both charged with high treason in Guildhall and, following torture of the prisoners, both were ajudged guilty though no proof had been established.

They were tortured again. Culpeper maintained the innocence of the Queen unswervingly to the last and nor could the extremity of torture draw from Derham an admission that the slightest criminality had passed between himself and Katharine since her marriage to the King.

However, on 6 December Damport, a 'friend' of Derham, admitted under torture that Derham had told him of his feelings towards Katharine and that he had fled to Ireland for the Queen's sake. Naturally Derham denied this, but to no avail.

Three days later Derham and Culpeper were taken to Tyburn, but Thomas, being of noble connections, was beheaded whilst Derham was hanged and quartered. Both protested their innocence until death finally took control of their racked bodies. The heads of both were placed on London Bridge.

On 21 January 1542 a bill for the attainder of Katharine Howard, late Queen of England, Lady Rochford, Agnes Howard Duchess of Norfolk, Lord Howard and others was produced. On 10 February Katharine was taken from Syon to the Tower and the following day Henry gave his consent to the bill which included the names of some of the victims whose heads already rotted above the Thames. Katharine was taken to the block on the morning of 13 February and submitted her head 'with meekness and courage' after only eighteen months of marriage.

Returning to Hollingbourne, let us recall that the ghost of the woman in the manor was described many years ago as wearing clothing of the sixteenth century so the figure could well be that of Katharine returning to the one house where, except for a few brief months with the King, she was really happy. Her ghost is known to exist in Hampton Court Palace and there is no reason at all why she should not haunt the two places where her emotions reached their maximum peak, one of utter joy and the other of soul-shattering fear.

At Eyhorne one can surely imagine the specialist worker

in the privacy of her small bedroom trying on one of her latest creations, twirling round in front of a mirror to admire the cut and the luxurious material which contrasted so strikingly with her own sombre grey gown. Perhaps it was here that she actually worked sitting in the corner to get the advantage of the evening sun to illuminate her needles and thread.

Could it be that one evening, whilst working perhaps on a dress for one of the Culpeper daughters, maybe even for the Queen herself, she learnt of the arrest of Thomas? A messenger had hurried from the manor house, running over the cinder path to give the urgent and dangerous news to all those connected with the Culpeper family.

What a shock that poor woman must have suffered, what emotional feelings of fright and terror filled that room. Thomas, the black sheep of the beloved family at the manor, was to be tortured and beheaded and the Queen's head was to follow, for the outcome of any trial in those days was obvious. Now everyone associated with the Culpepers was in danger of their lives.

Before her lay the roll of silk, evidence of her connections with the fated family. Would the material ever be used now? Did that poor frightened woman drag the material downstairs and hide it? Did she dare to take it back to the Culpepers, now trembling in anticipation of the result of their son's crime and foolishness? And is this what lies behind the haunting . . . or is there something worse?

CHAPTER 2

BOYS HALL,
WILLESBOROUGH

A few miles south of Ashford with its bustling and complicated traffic system, down a narrow twisting tree-lined road, lies the historical manor house of Boys Hall. The family responsible for the construction of this attractive home, the Bois or more likely de Bois, arrived from Normandy with William the Conqueror, but quickly settled down in what was then the sparsely populated area of south-east Kent.

Closely combined with the history of the family is that of the site itself, for it was during the Norman conquest that the first manor house of the area, then known as The Moat, was taken over by one of the Norman associates of the Bois family, Hugh de Montford.

The original buildings, shown on an old map of 1200 had actually belonged to the Convent of St Augustine but, as an ancient Saxon inheritance, passed to Sir John de Sevington during the reign of Edward III. The Sevingtons already held an adjoining manor according to Saxton's map of 1575 which also show a building at 'Broye' a few miles to the north. It seems likely that this might have been the original site of Boys Hall.

By 1361 Sir John de Barrie had assumed ownership through his marriage to Maud, only daughter of the Sevingtons. The Moat then passed, due to another marriage, to Vincent Boys of Bekesbourne. Vincent was the elder brother of the steward to five archbishops, thus strengthening the religious associations with the property even further. One notes that the anglicised version of the family name had by then become established.

For a short period John Alcock was the owner, but it returned to the Boys family as a result of the marriage of Thomas Boys of Mersham. From this gentleman's actions one gathers that parts of Kent, even in those early days, were subject to floods, perhaps from the River Stour which branched into the East and West Stour just south of Ashford, for it was Thomas who pulled down The Moat in 1616 and completely rebuilt it in 1632, using the original materials, on higher ground where it now stands. The moat of the original site still remains as a reminder of the earlier history.

To celebrate the 're-opening' of the house, the new owner named it Boys Hall. According to legend a secret tunnel was incorporated into the foundations and leads to Sevington Church. This may well be true in view of the religious attitude of the country at that time, but another suggestion for the use of the passageway was that it formed a route connecting the huge cellars with a hollow or cache in the grounds to facilitate smuggling wool out of the country and spirits into it. Alcoholic spirits of course.

Many of the fittings of Boys Hall are of the period of the seventeenth century, though not necessarily of the original building. Doors of Jacobean oak and two old linen-fold doors were found in a cellar of a house owned by a neighbour, but what oak panelling remains did once decorate the walls of The Moat.

Apparently at one time monks used at least one of the rooms which still retains a niche in the wall for holy relics and is now featured in what has become one of the bedrooms. A priest hole and secret stairway have unfortunately vanished, but there are still some puzzling aspects concerning the structure. At the top of the old English elm stairway on the left hand wall a single panel, framed by bevel-edged oak beams, suggests some other minute hiding place and some years ago, when the property was offered for sale, a prospective purchaser noted the exquisite panelling 'in the hall and dining-room'. On returning only a couple of days later to re-examine his possible buy there was no sign of this decoration. Even today some first time visitors comment on the glory of the panelling which has completely vanished when they return to take another look.

But it was a series of incidents during the eighteenth century which have affected the life in Boys Hall ever since.

A New Years Eve party had been arranged and guests were beginning to arrive. The squire from Chart who had ridden over with his cousin, Mr Toke, from Willesborough and the Radcliffes from Ashford in their new coach, were a few of the characters involved in what was to be a case of murder.

Already in the house to welcome the friends and neighbours were of course Mr and Mrs Boys, and their son Lieutenant William Boys, a captain in the Royal Marines, their daughter Elizabeth and two other guests Ellen Scott and someone called Tracy, whose christian name was never recorded. It is unfortunate that little is known of Tracy for he was to figure very prominently in the future events.

Elizabeth Boys, seventeen years old and just left school, had announced her engagement to a young man 'whose genial mood and comliness fairly attoned for his lack of brains'. Her friend Ellen, the other chief character in the case, was 'a determined young female but was a mere child in appearance'. She was the sole survivor of a family all of whom are buried in the churchyard at Brabourne, and had also declared her betrothal to the son of the house.

Her fiancé, the tall Lieutenant Boys, had already seen some active service in India and was obviously considered as a 'great catch' by the girl.

The general excitement of welcoming the guests had died down and the small groups and clusters of people drifted into the drawing room for sherry and gossip. At 4 o'clock dinner was announced.

After a magnificent feast amidst the joyful atmosphere of

a typical Christmas at the Hall, the guests were directed upstairs to the main withdrawing-room where further entertainment awaited.

The room had been well prepared. Huge chandeliers provided their warm and sparkling brilliance, logs burnt merrily in the huge fireplace and the boards had been well waxed in readiness for the dancing that was to follow. The enthusiasm of the guests to partake in the overall merriment and party spirit was evidenced by Mrs Radcliffe whose feet became so hot that she had, 'amidst much laughter', abandoned her shoes for they had become stuck to the floor. She continued her dancing with unabated energy.

Finally the exhausted guests sat down to enjoy further gossip, much needed liquid refreshment and, when partially recovered, to a game at the card table.

Ellen had noted with poorly hidden pleasure that the handsome young Tracy had been constantly smiling at her and paying so many compliments that she had frequently blushed with embarrassment. The couple, quietly sitting in a corner away from the main crowd, chatted and discussed a myriad of topics. Perhaps because of the atmosphere of friendly homeliness, perhaps because of the obvious neglect of her fiancé, Ellen began to realise that her feelings towards the young man facing her were strengthening. The fact that she had known him but a few hours and that she was engaged to an army officer, seemed to mean nothing. He was so handsome, so bright and cheerful, so knowledgeable about women and their problems.

A Sir Roger de Coverley was suggested and as Tracy asked her for the pleasure of the dance the girl felt her heart pound with excitement. Her partner held her close, too close. The couple wafted over the floor like lovers, she gazing adoringly into his eyes, he clasping her firmly and yet with tenderness.

Was it just the heat of the room or was it the drink that made the girl feel so giddy? Tracy failed to notice the weakening of his partner and suddenly, with a gasp, Ellen fainted in his arms. Shocked and worried, he carried her gently to a nearby settee, laid her down and asked for smelling salts to be obtained. The guests rushed over to the couple, deeply concerned, but one was more worried than the others. Lieutenant Boys stood glowering down at the unconscious body of his fiancée and then glanced at Tracy. There was no need for words, his expression of hate was only too evident.

William bent down and administered the smelling bottle. Ellen began to recover but, still slightly faint, took his hand. 'Oh Tracy, Tracy', she murmured. The officer tried to disguise his feelings of intense anger as he stood up pulling his hand away. 'She is coming to herself.'

Minutes later the girl had fully recovered but the atmosphere in the room, or at least in that particular corner, had turned cold.

The incident had caused an awkward feeling of general embarrassment and the guests used this as an excuse to make preparations for their departure. But someone suddenly realised that the hour of midnight had passed without notice and attempts were made, amidst cries of 'Happy New Year', to rejuvenate the cheerful atmosphere of a few minutes earlier. It was only partially successful, although 'Auld Lang Syne' was sung with great fervour.

Finally the party began to break up and couples moved downstairs to collect their cloaks. A young voice called out:

> 'For he who opens first the door
> To let the New Year tread the floor
> Shall see misfortune at the fore.'

Mr Toke responded in his normal way to such 'old wives tales' and murmured 'rubbish' to all and sundry. Tracy shouted: 'Who cares anyway?' and, flinging open the heavy door with an extravagant gesture of raising both arms, bellowed: 'Welcome to the New Year!'

The guests had all departed. The house was still. In the drawing room Ellen was sitting on the sofa with William, trying rationally to persuade him to release her from the bond of marriage. Her arguments were failing. He was adamant. But she no longer loved him. He couldn't love her in the circumstances. It was not his fault . . .

Reasons, excuses, pleadings were to no avail. He was an army officer. The contract had been made and would be kept. He had a reputation, they both had. Think of the family. No, the marriage will take place. And take place it did.

Nine years passed, in which time the household completely changed and the whole picture was altered.

Mr Boys, the elder, was dead and Elizabeth his daughter, after being crippled in an accident, had also died. William, having married Ellen, had been posted back to India and then Egypt where he was killed in a local skirmish. An occasional report had filtered through to England for a few weeks after the wedding telling friends and relatives that the marriage was an unhappy union and should never have taken place. Then the messages had ceased and nothing more was heard. The family sadly assumed that Ellen had died in the Sudan.

Of Tracy there had been no sign since the party and it was felt that he too had gone abroad to forget. He was certainly absent from the wedding ceremony.

Snow had come early to Kent; on 22 December Boys Hall shivered in its white embrace. The only occupants were the family retainers, old servants and a cousin who now lived peacefully by herself with her memories. Voices and activity in the old house were quiet and subdued. It was as if the hall was in partial hibernation.

Suddenly a knock at the front door roused the household. 'Was that a knock . . . on a night like this . . . who could it be . . . ?' The snow already lay thick on the lawns and was still falling fast. The group in the servants' quarters were silent, straining to hear another noise, another clue as to the caller. A weird pitiful moan, a heart-rending sob and a further knock, louder this time, broke the stillness.

A maid ran to the door. There stood the frail bedraggled figure of Ellen Boys. With snowflakes covering her thin gown, the same gown that she had worn to a party nine years ago, she stood swaying weakly in the doorway. With glazed eyes she murmured, 'He has been calling me. I've been walking round for such a long time. I can't find him. No, not William, he's dead. Tracy. It's Tracy. Look . . . '

She thrust a crumpled scrap of paper towards the young servant who, with trembling hand, opened it and read, 'My darling, it is not too late. My love is fire compared with icy heart . . . '

Whilst the girl read the message Ellen staggered into the hallway to be greeted by her joyous cousin. No questions would she answer, but just brushed her relatives aside and stumbled feverishly up the stairs.

The women in the hall looked upwards, whispering together and shaking their heads. It was obvious Ellen had lost her mind, but where had she been and what was she talking about? Her voice could be heard crying out, 'He is hiding from me. Tracy, where are you?'

Suddenly an awful scream caused them to rush together up the wide stairway to a small bedroom leading off the corridor, at the other end of which lay a room which had nine years previously been used for a New Year's party.

The group stopped in the doorway of the small room, horrified at the sight which met their gaze. Ellen stood looking with wild mad eyes at the floor. She had moved two heavy chests and torn up with bare fingers three floorboards. Torn, bleeding skin and the broken nails of her hands showed with what strength and insane power she had worked. She was swaying and murmuring, an idiotic smile on her lips.

'There! I knew he was hiding from me. For months I have called him and he answered.' She turned to face the wide-eyed scared women in the doorway. 'He did. He answered, but his voice grew weaker and more feeble. Tracy, my love, why are you there? Why don't you answer?'

An old gardener who had been quickly summoned pushed his way through the group and kneeled down to examine the aperture in the floor. Lying awkwardly between the rough joists was the skeleton of a body still wearing the clothes worn by Tracy on that fateful night. The old man gently put his gnarled hand under the skull to raise it and, with a 'click', a bullet fell on to the stained plaster beneath.

Before anyone could stop her, the crazed woman bent down and seizing the small piece of lead, ran to the loft window where the baleful moonlight offered a better view of the object. Turning the fatal relic round in her fingers she staggered and fell, crashing through the window to a silent death 20ft below.

After what seemed hours later Dr Whitfield arrived and, having dealt with the shattered form of Ellen, declared the need for a coroners' verdict on the remains of the body beneath the floor. But the declaration he made as he examined the skeleton stunned those around him into a disbelieving and incredulous silence. 'Those bones,' he said as he stood up, 'are those of a woman.'

Days of bewilderment followed the tragedy. The coroner, however, was to confirm the doctor's findings in that Tracy had been a woman. Ellen and the remains of the other body were buried together in one coffin in Chantry Chapel, under a stone inscribed 'We see through a glass darkly'.

There is another slightly different version of the story relating to the two 'lovers', in which Ellen committed suicide by jumping through the window, but after 200 years it is impossible to be certain of the truth. The important fact remains that Ellen died, and died tragically. Both she and Tracy died in tragic circumstances and the mental disturbance of that event must live on in the structure of the building. Yet at first glance there is little to provide a connection with that pitiful saga of the 1700s with the experiences of the twentieth century.

Between 1970 and 1973 a team of workmen were employed

to carry out a vast renovation programme of Boys Hall. Every member of that group during that period saw, what appeared to them to be, a 'white smock or shirt' glide silently along a path at the side of the building. None of them were able to describe the garment more fully because it was seen for such a short time, 'just fleetingly', and nobody could say whether there was anything below the smock. Representatives from the local electricity board confirmed the phenomena.

It has also been seen travelling past the sitting-room window and past one of the kitchens of the eastern wing. The left arm of the garment is slashed exposing a bare arm, but whether that of a male or female no one can tell.

The ghost of someone in white or light grey clothing has also been seen standing by the lake in the grounds on more than one occasion, but when approached or pointed out to someone else the figure just vanishes.

Regular footsteps are frequently heard walking along the corridor and down the stairs to the first landing and similar noises heard in the stables. So distinct were they on one occasion that Roger, a friend of the family, turned round to say 'hello' but the building was empty.

Other sounds of some invisible entity with 'a heavy tread' have been heard walking through empty bedrooms and doorways now sealed up and even opening and closing non-existent doors.

A previous housekeeper claimed that she frequently heard scratchings of a dog at a bedroom door and two of the workmen admitted that they had heard the sounds of a dog padding through the former kitchen, now a sitting-room, when working on the restoration project.

Mrs Vera Akers, wife of the owner of Boys Hall, is, perhaps surprisingly, a little disappointed at not witnessing more phenomena. When polishing in the main bedroom one afternoon she felt a hand placed firmly on her shoulder and, thinking it was one of her daughters, turned round to greet her. But no one was there.

The only other occasion that inexplicable entities have demonstrated their power to Mrs Akers was in 1972 when, while making a bed, she turned at hearing a noise behind her to see her transistor radio slowly move from the top of a vanity unit, cross the room and land with a crash on the floor a few feet away.

In the same room, where guests have heard footsteps walking through the partition wall, an English friend from Arabia mentioned the sighing, heavy breathing and banging that she heard whilst sleeping there.

Richard, a painter, told me that on the day before my visit he had been working on the bannisters at the top of the stairway when he heard a bedroom door open and footsteps walk along the corridor. 'Without looking up I said good morning, Mrs Akers', but getting no reply he raised his eyes and realised that the corridor was empty even though the sounds were continuing and went round a corner of a wall. 'Most eerie,' he commented.

Those steps of invisible walkers could, one supposes, be any one of hundreds of previous occupiers, although the present owner believes that there is some connection between these sounds and the finding of a gold hoard of coins in the hallway in the early days of the renovation. The fourteen coins, covering the period from Edward III to George III, had been discovered by a carpenter in a stone pot beneath the rotting floorboards.

It is perhaps more likely that the experience of the overseas guest can provide some link with the murder of Tracy and the resultant suicide.

A man, having carried the dead body of a woman from the murder site with the intention of placing it in an aperture below the flooring, would naturally be breathing fairly heavily. The sounds of hammering back the floorboards are likely in the circumstances and under the strong emotion of that moment might easily imprint themselves, at least for a considerable period, on the atmosphere of the room.

So who was the murderer? One supposes it must have been William Boys, but a prolonged absence after the party would have been noticed and associated with the absence of Tracy. So who wears a smock and would have a dog which would follow him wherever he went? The gardener is a good candidate.

He is an old faithful servant, disturbed at the turn of events on that critical day, who surely would be willing to comply with the wishes of 'the young master' to carry out 'the foul deed' and even hide the body. Perhaps in the fight with his victim the sleeve of his smock was torn. Was he paid, paid with fourteen gold coins which, feeling unable to take the 'blood money' straight away, he hid beneath the floor of the hall? Why was the old gardener the first man to come to that fatal room? It has been said that a murderer always returns to the scene of his crime. Did he? We will never know.

Despite the appearances of the bodyless smock, the continuing sounds of footsteps of an unseen entity, the phantom dog and the appalling mystery surrounding Ellen's love for Tracy, Boys Hall exudes an atmosphere of absolute content and comfort.

Beneath one of the largest mulberry trees in the south one can sit admiring the soft green swath of the lawns, the attractive lines of the sunken garden and perhaps take comfort in the thought that had Ellen ever discovered the truth about her amour, her mind would have been even more disturbed. At least Mrs Radcliffe enjoyed that evening of mystery 200 years ago.

CHAPTER 3

GLEBE HOUSE, FOLKESTONE

An ancient fort known as Caesar's Camp shows that the excellence of Folkestone as a military site has been appreciated since pre-Roman times. But until the railways acquired the port in 1842 the town itself had little significance other than that of a centre for smugglers.

Shorncliffe Camp, well known throughout the country by those called up for national service in the last war, actually dates back to the Crimean war and covers about six hundred acres of the Kent countryside. The major part of one of the outlying properties owned by the military authorities was originally built in 1840 and was called Lord Beechborough House. Today it is called by another name and for the sake of security I will call it 'The Glebe House'.

I first heard of the haunting when providing a series of lectures at the Adult Education Centre on the subject of ghost-hunting. One of the students provided so much information about the property that it sounded as if it were challenging Borley Rectory as the most haunted house in England.

A few weeks later, owing to the kindness of various officers, I stood in front of the derelict empty house looking at its square lines, the white cement facing cracking with age and the boarded up windows. Even in the bright sunshine the house emitted some peculiar atmosphere of dread and of silent horror.

No birds sang, no insects buzzed, nothing moved. Encroaching weeds, already entwining one wall of the crumbling porchway, seemed only to heighten the silence which covered the area like an unseen muffling and frightening blanket.

It was here in this house of mystery that shortly before World War I a young lieutenant, distraught with worry over his outstanding debts worsened by excessive gambling, had seen the brigade commander asking for advice and, if possible, assistance. The brigadier, rigid with generations of army discipline behind him, merely suggested that there was only one way out for such a foolish young officer.

From a service family myself, my uncle a colonel and my nephew a major, I can well imagine the sort of comment that the commander would have made. 'If you cannot control your own affairs you cannot be expected to control those of others. You are no use, sir, to the British Army. You have but one way out for the disgrace you have brought upon the Regiment. You have the means . . . I only hope for your own sake and that of the Army you have the courage.'

In those days army life was hard. There was no compassion, no sympathy, no understanding for personal mistakes or errors committed by any officer young or old. It shows that the lieutenant himself must have been really desperate to think of approaching not just his company commander but the general in command of the brigade.

But, as one would expect, the door would be closed on the matter and the young man left to reach his own solution. There was only one. He took his revolver from its holster, checked the safety catch and chamber and, standing in the centre of the entrance hall, placed the barrel of the weapon to his head and squeezed the trigger.

How the official army records dealt with the sad event can only be surmised. No doubt an 'accidental death' was recorded by the Court of Enquiry for suicides are unpopular in any regiment.

The building and its inhabitants ignored the disturbance. Glebe House continued to be used as the brigadier's headquarters, but in 1932 another incident was to affect the atmosphere.

I opened the front door and predictably it creaked. Stepping over the broken floor tiles of the porch I entered the silent hall, stopped and shivered. Paper faded with age clung limply to the walls, in places unsuccessfully and peeled away revealing cracked plaster beneath. Chipped paint on the doors and skirting, bare scratched floorboards—all merged into a picture of dismal desertion.

Looking into every room on the ground floor I gained an impression not of sadness but of cold efficiency, of heartless neutrality. I moved into the dining-room with its french windows looking out at the side of the house to the lawns and magnificent view of the countryside across the cow-dotted fields to the sea beyond. Here was a feeling of joviality, the sound of clinking glasses and of merriment and yet to my senses it seemed forced. A façade for the benefit of some special visitor perhaps, or was it just the usual attitude of making such events appear to be happy occasions regardless of undercurrents of worry, concern and even misery?

On one specific day in 1932 this room would have been busy with staff preparing for the usual dinner for guests of the brigadier. Maids would be carefully laying the tables, whilst the stewards in their immaculate uniforms moved rapidly here and there checking glasses, wine and cigar stocks.

Upstairs chambermaids would be preparing the bedrooms for guests whilst the general's batman busily occupied himself with his officer's uniform for the night. Underlying this activity, however, that batman and one of those maids were thinking of other things, of other far more personal problems which were to explode into a tragedy that few were to forget that night or for many nights to come.

The day's activity was over. The local guests had departed and those from a distance had retired for the night. A few of the living-in servants were still clearing away the final remnants of the dinner. The batman, having already prepared

35

the officer's uniform for the morning parade and laid out the orders for attention in the office, was steeling himself for an unpleasant scene.

For some months he had been enjoying a quiet but satisfying affair with one of the more attractive chambermaids, but recently he had heard rumours from associates that 'his girl' had been 'playing around' with one of the other men on the staff. That night he was to 'have it out with her'.

Having consumed perhaps just a shade too much 'Dutch courage' he stumbled to her room.

The girl lying in her small bed was apprehensive. She knew her man must have heard about her foolish activities with someone else, but felt perhaps that with her usual guile he would forgive and forget or even, she hoped, accept her denials. The man was standing beside her now cursing her as a 'whore', a 'slut', a cheap harlot. His anger rose as she protested and her appeals were ignored. He stormed, he raged. The girl's voice rose now in anger. She was not engaged to him, she could do what she liked.

Something snapped in the man's mind and he fell on to the quaking figure, hands gripping her throat in abject violent fury. His fingers squeezed that white unresisting throat until it seemed it would burst from the inhuman pressure. Suddenly the man realised the figure beneath him was quiet and still. The girl's eyes and tongue protruded horribly and her face was tinged with blue.

He staggered back, apalled at what he had done. Murder! The word flashed into his mind and hung like the rope which he knew now awaited him. Phrases of excuse came. 'I didn't mean it. I was drunk. It was an accident.' None sounded genuine. He knew his end.

His brigadier, having heard the commotion, appeared in the doorway. His face was rigid. Nothing was said. Words were not needed. He looked at his batman. 'Go to your room.' The man obeyed like a zombie. The officer closed the door, locked it and removed the key methodically.

He followed his batman and repeated the process, locking the servant into his own quarters. Quietly so that his guests would not be disturbed, unemotionally because he was a senior officer, he returned to his own room, went to bed and to sleep.

One can only imagine the thoughts of the murderer. His conscience would have given him no peace that night. Every minute of those moments of uncontrolled anger would be imprinted on his memory for ever. He tossed and turned, his mind racked with the crime, with excuses and with hopes.

The morning came and he heard the sounds of voices outside. He staggered to the window to look down on the group of civilian police as they gathered in the unfamiliar courtyard. He heard the brigadier come to his door, unlock it and swing it open. 'Come on. They are waiting for you.' The order was as brusque and as unemotional as usual.

What could the man do, could he run? There was nowhere to run to. The officer went down the main staircase to advise the police that the soldier was coming, but the murderer, realising his predicament, ran quickly to the adjoining bedroom and grabbed the revolver which he knew would be there. Quickly he slipped a couple of bullets into the chamber and ran unthinkingly to the service stairs at the back of the house.

He didn't know really why he took this action or what he intended to do. He was half-way down the narrow stairway leading to the kitchen when he realised that several police were standing by the pantry door. It was no good. There was no escape. The only outcome would be 'the rope'—an ignoble ending for an officer's batman. Training and rigid discipline took control. The young man stood still and upright. One hand was clenched by his side, the other holding the officer's revolver moved to his head and with a deep breath he squeezed the trigger. The loud report brought the police crashing through the door, but it was too late.

As I walked slowly up that narrow darkened stairway I had to stop at one point to look back at the dim shadowy pantry. At this point the temperature dropped suddenly and I felt the hairs at the back of my head tingle. I shivered and continued moving upwards. A few yards away, on the right hand side, a small bedroom lay at the end of a narrow corridor. It was in here, I was told, that the chambermaid met her death.

All that remained was a wardrobe with one of the doors hanging awkwardly half off its frame, a dusty empty shelf and a few indentations on the floor showing where the girl's bed had stood. It was cold and austere.

I moved back into the main corridor and turned to reach another tragic spot. A short passageway faced me and I entered, passing on my right what I thought was a cupboard. It was pitch dark but larger than just a storage area. It was an airing cupboard fitted with the usual shelving, but high up near the ceiling a large water supply pipe crossed the tiny room.

Within living memory an army padre, a lieutenant-colonel, was found hanging from that pipe!

There is a possible reason for his drastic action. The government of the day had decided to reduce the number of regiments in the army for economic reasons. One of the units to be affected was that of the colonel's. It was to be merged with another, losing its identity, and in his mind perhaps also its unique history, traditions and individuality. Feeling, as he probably did, that he formed an integral part of the living regiment, it would be difficult for him to accept the situation and despite his overall affection for army life it would be impossible to continue as merely another supernumerary officer, 'excess to requirements'.

Two days before the official amalgamation ceremony the officer took the final step and another case of suicide was added to the history of the Glebe House.

Continuing my tour of the creepy silent building, I entered

another bedroom facing out onto the front drive. Although no known tragedy has occurred in this room within the last fifty years, two young girls sleeping in the room stated that they had seen a soldier come from out of the wall and glide quickly out into the corridor. Could this phantom have been that of the batman rushing out with the revolver stolen from the brigadier? Later, when working in the bathroom in the passageway adjoining the airing cupboard, one of the charladies heard footsteps along the corridor and realising that the house should have been empty went to investigate. She was just in time to see the figure of a woman slip into the same room, but when she arrived the bedroom was empty. Was this a visit from the murdered chambermaid? Dogs are reluctant to move up the main stairs of the house and they flatly refuse to enter that particular bedroom.

At one time, fairly recently, Glebe House was used as a hostel for students cared for by a colonel's daughter and a 'general help', the only two people who had keys to the property. It was during this period that one of the most puzzling incidents occurred.

One morning when all the students were out training, a laundry basket was delivered. Being too heavy for the women to carry upstairs at that moment, it was left at the bottom of the stairs to await assistance from the young lads. The ladies left, locking the front door. At 4pm they returned only to find the basket had disappeared.

The couple searched the entire ground floor without success. Realising that the laundry basket couldn't just vanish, the officer's daughter went up to the first floor and was astonished to find it outside the airing cupboard. How a basket, too heavy for three people to lift, found its way up the stairs, across the corridor and into the passageway is utterly beyond comprehension. But it is not an isolated incident.

In October 1974, three visitors to the empty house, having examined the whole structure, were about to depart down the stairs when a lamp bulb tinkled on to the floor of the corridor behind them. The first puzzling aspect was why the delicate glass had not broken on the bare wood of the floorboards and the second was the source of the bulb itself.

Other inexplicable incidents have occurred in the dining-room.

A young lady responsible for the house in the early 1970s was preparing, with the assistance of a waitress, for an important dinner for a group of executives. The table was laid, but shortly before the arrival of the guests the cutlery was checked. Although both ladies involved had been working together for some time and were used to dealing with such occasions, the senior was puzzled to see that forks and spoons of two place settings were missing. They had been there when the table was originally laid so a general hunt was made and every item doubly checked, but to no avail. Replacement cutlery was finally obtained and the two places relaid. The guests began to arrive and the hostess, having conducted them to the lounge for aperitifs, just popped her head round the dining-room door to ensure all was well and was astounded to see that again two places were devoid of the necessary cutlery. A further set of replacements was called for and the dinner proceeded without further problems.

It seems as though whenever the house is full of people there is a strong feeling of resentment which pervades the dining-room, the kitchen and the larder.

Miss Anderson, when working in the food preparation area on one occasion, was so certain that someone had joined her in the kitchen that she turned round, greeting them with a friendly 'hello', but the room was empty.

I returned to the ground floor to examine the pantry and the game larder in more detail. Both rooms were icy cold, but I assumed the reason to be the existence of drains beneath the floor.

Walking back into the dining-room I noticed a small built-in cupboard in one wall beside the french doors. On opening the door I found myself in a small wine cellar, empty except for the racks which for decades would have held a magnificent selection of high quality wines for the delight of the numerous guests.

One day in September 1973, Mrs Bannister was quietly setting up the tables in preparation for one of the regular dinners; she glanced over towards the cellar and stifled a scream. The door was ajar and in the space was the half-hidden figure of 'an old man in a pepper and salt suit bending towards the racks'.

The frightened woman called out to her colleague, Miss Anderson, who came running just in time to hear Mrs Bannister say, 'He's gone. The figure just vanished.'

Was this partly seen phantom that of the lieutenant-colonel who might well have decided to bolster his courage before committing his personal crime? The absence of uniform is not remarkable if we consider that he was off duty and in his own home; the more popular type of country gentlemen's suit would be conventional 'mufti'.

The coincidence regarding the vanished cutlery is striking for it was the only time that two sets from two places were ever missed. The peculiar factor is that both the officers who committed suicide would, at some time or other, have sat at that table.

The atmosphere in the room was different now. No longer was there the sense of false geniality, but a feeling of efficiency, perhaps of a definite resolution having been made affecting the future of a family and that of a man's life. I could well imagine that it was in this room that the final fatal decision was made.

I looked round expecting to see a cocktail cabinet against a wall, a long table set for sixteen or more people, but the room was empty. There was only a pane of cracked glass in one of the french doors, some paper curling away from the wall, and an empty lamp socket hanging bare and forlorn. The room was resentful of people, like a man who, drained of other emotion, can yet focus hate on those he believes are to blame for his situation.

I could not help sighing as the room seemed to sigh, as the house itself seemed to sigh. Unanswerable questions remained. Who lifted the laundry basket up the stairs? Who threw a lamp bulb on to the floor of the corridor? Who 'stole' two sets of forks and spoons?

As I closed the front door I breathed in the sunshine and warmth and comfort of a summer's day, thankful that the old days of rigid discipline have vanished . . . forever?

CHAPTER 4

OLD SOAR, PLAXTOL

In the centre of the hop fields of Kent, adjoining a pair of glorious converted oast houses, one finds the medieval house of Old Soar, partially hidden by a wall and surrounding trees. Described as one of the most notable survivors of thirteenth-century domestic architecture, it is situated some two miles from the village of Plaxtol on the side of a small hill between Ightham, with its haunted mote, and Mereworth.

The medieval section of the building, the part open to the public, dates from 1290 and comprises a solar, a chapel and a second room with garderobe. The solar, orginally used as a bedsitting-room by the lord of the manor, rests on a barrel-vaulted undercroft. Attached to it is an eighteenth-century privately owned brick farm house built on the foundations of the thirteenth-century aisled hall which was destroyed by fire in the 1600s.

Very little is known about the inhabitants who lived, died or haunt Old Soar, but belief is that it belonged to a branch of the famous Colepepper family. It was the action of one of them, William, that resulted in Old Soar being given its name.

William Colepepper, custodian of Leeds Castle, had received a request for admittance in 1321 from Queen Isabella, wife of Edward II, but for some reason or other he refused. This rejection may have been a form of protest against the King, one of the most unpopular sovereigns in English history owing to his love of personal pleasure and devoted attachment to favourite courtiers. However, the castle was attacked, and

William executed only a year before Edward himself was brutally murdered in Berkeley Castle by Sir Thomas Gurney and Sir John Maltravers in September 1327.

William's mother named Old Soar to perpetuate her distress, *soar* being Norman for 'grief', but the family continued to gain wealth, power and property, primarily as a result of their habit of kidnapping heiresses and forcibly marrying them. At one time they were the largest landowning family in the whole of Kent and Sussex.

The first reference to Old Soar is on William's death in 1326 when up to then it had been owned by the branch of the family living at Preston near Aylesford.

Some people think that Sir Thomas Culpeper stayed at Old Soar when touring the area to lecture to midwives, but this is rather unlikely for it was Nicholas who was the medical expert and he died in 1654. The two Thomas's, father and son, were more interested in the problems of lending money, both having written treatises on usury. The elder died in 1662 and the younger in 1697.

Eventually the house became part of the estate of the Geary family, but on the death of Sir William Geary Mrs S. L. Cannon gained ownership and in 1947 she presented it to the National Trust. Since then the Department of the Environment have maintained and preserved it.

The eighteenth century with its religious revivals, not to mention the wars and general strife, resulted in one of the most important rooms in any sufficiently large house being the private chapel, which often doubled up as a study. The lord of the manor would transact business there during the day, whilst in the evenings he would carry out his devotions with the family and perhaps hold a small service joined by a few friends.

Here children of the family would be christened and baptised and occasionally a wedding ceremony would excite the whole village.

Beneath the chapel in its vaulted basements would be

stored the family's valuables, clothing materials and luxuries bought in the annual fairs. Because it was not until the eighteenth century that the growing of root crops was introduced so that the herds of cattle could be kept during the winter, proceeds of the harvest and salted meat would also be stored in the undercroft.

Hunting was not just an excuse for a popular pastime but provided a valuable change from the salted meat, and to vary the food even more there was usually a dovecote or pigeon house. There is an excellent example of a working dovecote complete with a moving ladder at Dunster in Somerset.

Let us imagine, then, life in those days. It was rural, somewhat frugal, especially for the servants and the farm workers. They got up with the sunrise to a hard day's toil in the fields or the kitchen, and returned at sunset to their cottages tired and weary. Entertainment would have consisted of rather crude forms of cricket and football played on a convenient village green, and perhaps a monthly visit to the local fair or market.

One of the dairymaids employed on the home farm by the Geary family, a girl thought to be named Jenny, was one of the quieter girls among the community. She would be a pleasant enough character but rather shy and reserved, perhaps slightly 'simple', otherwise she would have been employed inside the house.

Let's imagine the situation which may be the cause of the phenomena.

The girl, about seventeen years of age, had fallen in love with Edward, one of the other farm workers, but unfortunately the affection was rather one-sided. The man, known as Edward to Jenny but Ted to his 'mates', was about ten years older than the dairymaid and, unlike the girl, was ambitious. Light relief from his toil on the farm would be provided by a few frolics in the fields with Jenny who was, to his mind, merely a 'fringe benefit'. She didn't pester him about marriage, worry him for money or for clothes and presents, but just seemed satisfied with the occasional visits to the local hostelry.

Ted lived with his widowed mother, in one of the workmen's cottage's in Plaxtol. Jenny and her father were housed in one of the farm cottages on the estate.

The girl's father, churlish and morose after the loss of his wife in childbirth, had little or no love for his daughter who, in his view, had caused the death of her mother. What had hurt him even more was the dawning realisation that the girl was what we would term 'mentally retarded', and was looked on as the village simpleton.

He had tried to beat some sense into Jenny but to no avail —she was just worthless and stupid. Despite her father's behaviour, his moods, his drunkenness, Jenny loved him. Having experienced no maternal love she directed her simple affection at the only two men she really knew.

She was a shapely and attractive wench and had been playfully pursued by several of the other farm workers, but they had merely teased and jeered at her when she rejected their advances. Edward on the other hand had, she considered, treated her 'like a woman'. She never entertained ideas of marriage, that was for real ladies, but had been delighted to receive small gifts from 'her man'. These presents would only be cheap baubles from the local fair or a bunch of wild roses culled from the hedgerows, but to her they were jewels and bouquets. It took little to make her happy.

As Christmas approached the usual preparations were being made for the annual festivities in the house, but it was 1775 and the country was in a pitiful state. The foreign wars, duty on imported corn and the poor harvest raised the price of bread to a prohibitive rate. Meat and foodstuffs were equally expensive and low wages for the workers made it difficult for enthusiasm to be excessive. Bread was 1s a loaf, but those who baked it received a mere 9d a week. A carpenter earned 1s for six days' work; mutton was 10½d and beef 1s per lb and the result was an increase in the amount of drunkenness and starvation all over the country.

Despite being part of a hop-growing and farming community the Gearys at Old Soar were hard put to it to provide anything like the usual Christmas fare and were ashamed at the sparse table that was to be offered that year to their friends. However, they were determined to put 'a good face on it'. Holly, ivy, mistletoe, rosemary, bay,—indeed anything colourful—was brought in to decorate the building, though evergreens, of course, would not be used before Christmas Eve.

Jenny and her colleagues were as busy as ever making cheese, butter and cream in the dairy whilst Ted, her father and the other men would be striving to provide the meat and liquor.

The day arrived and the guests welcomed, but the servants and farm workers were to have no rest. More beer, more venison. The rich were unconcerned as to where the provisions came from, the appearance of joviality and wealth had to be kept up.

Partly because of the shortage of food, sickness had reduced the number of work force available for that Christmas so Jenny was hard-pressed to keep pace with the continuing demands for 'more butter and more cream'. The day drew near its close and guests, many of them suffering from over-indulgence, were staggering about the house shouting, singing, squealing with uninhibited delight. They had enjoyed a marvellous traditional meal complete with wine and huge quantities of locally brewed ale.

The young family priest, stumbling through the kitchen, saw Jenny arriving with another bowl of thick cream. 'Hello, my girl. You're a pretty young wench. Come over here.'

Jenny, scared at being approached in this way by one of 'the gentlemen', especially one of the clergy, put down the container and stood still. A couple of serving maids giggled whilst the cook admonished them, telling them to get on with their work.

'Come here, my lass,' said the man and staggered towards the dairymaid.

'No sir,' she said and ran out, back towards the dairy. But the befuddled mind of her pursuer now contained only thoughts of Jenny and her body. It was Christmas, a time for everyone to enjoy themselves. Finally he found the girl shivering with fright in one of the barns.

'Ha! There you are, my dear. Now you'll be kind to me, won't you?'

Poor Jenny, scared to call out or protest, let the young drunken fool have his way.

Time passed and midsummer arrived. The house and farm had forgotten Christmas, but not Jenny for, as a result of that frightening incident in the barn, she was pregnant. Edward, puzzled and worried, had been less frequent in his visits whilst her father had stormed and raged, accusing her of being the village idiot.

What was she to do? It would only be a few months now before the baby arrived and only she knew the father. She wouldn't go to 'the master' for he wouldn't believe her. She was only a stupid dairymaid. Her father ignored her and Edward had deserted her. What or who was left?

She had only one recourse: to see the father in his chapel.

It was a Sunday afternoon. She knew the man would be there. Miserable and dejected, she slowly climbed the spiral staircase of the hall. She had little confidence in the priest. What could he do? He couldn't and certainly wouldn't marry her. Edward had left her, her father didn't want her. No one wanted her now.

Jenny, poor Jenny, at last reached the top of the stairs and stood panting and recovering from the exertion. She heard the priest practising on the small organ in the chapel. Quietly she crossed the floor to the doorway at the corner of the room. She saw a long grey dark cloak hanging on the wall of the chapel and, taking a deep breath, entered. The priest had stopped playing and was standing silently looking down at the piscina, the stone basin used to hold the water to purify the chalice.

As the girl entered the holy room he turned and in one glance realised the reason for her visit. After telling her to sit down on one of the chairs, he started to pace the floor backwards and forwards. The room was silent except for the sound of those footsteps. Jenny dared not speak and the man found he could hardly think—the girl was in trouble because of him—could he bluff his way out? Could he perhaps persuade someone else to marry her and take the responsibility?

He racked his brains, pacing the floor with worry about his position, for the girl and her child, their child. If the 'master' discovered the secret he would be de-frocked. He could not leave the church. He was a Catholic and had little or no money anyway.

Reaching a decision he sat down to face the trembling, white-faced girl. He explained his problems, suggested a quiet marriage with her boy friend, 'she had got a boy friend?' and told her to come regularly to confession, where he could give her words of spiritual comfort.

The girl continued to look at him in silence. What could she say? The priest, hopefully, got up, telling the girl to think about his words, to seriously consider the situation for the sake of the child and her soul. Taking one more glance at that sorrowful little figure sitting alone, alone in the world, the hypocrite walked away and down the stairway.

Jenny sat there for some minutes. She had said nothing. She looked round the room and glanced at the bowl of water.

Distraught with worry, she had been unable to touch any food that morning and hunger, her condition and her state of mind combined together to produce a terrible faintness. The room began to sway before her. She rose shakily and moved towards the piscina thinking water would revive her. The faintness increased, she reeled and stumbled. Her head smacked against the side of the bowl and her face broke the surface of the water.

An hour later the priest returned to find Jenny dead. Having knocked herself unconscious she had drowned in a mere couple of inches of water. Ironically, it was holy water.

Thus Jenny died, accidentally. But even though it is hard to imagine someone committing suicide by this method, the villagers assumed this to be the case and, as a result, her body was buried in unconsecrated ground.

In 1971 the caretaker for the trustees was asked whether she knew Old Soar was haunted by 'the ghost of an eighteenth-century dairymaid who committed suicide in the chapel because she had got herself into trouble'. 'No,' was the reply. 'I've only just moved down here and have no knowledge of anything about the building yet.' The visitor claimed that he had frequently seen lights in the empty building and a friend had heard the sound of music coming from the chapel.

Guests of the owners of the adjoining farm house, sitting in the long room abutting the solar, also enquired about the source of the 'church music' that they heard issuing through the wall. 'We thought the old part of the house was empty,' they said. It had been.

On a Sunday in June a year later a young couple visiting Old Soar asked about 'the ghost in the chapel'. They knew there was one there because 'it suddenly went very cold'. The following Sunday another pair of visitors also commented about the 'cold ghostly feeling in the chapel'.

One evening during the same month, but the following year, the caretaker checking over the solar glanced towards the chapel and saw a 'long grey dark cloak hanging from the wall'. By the time she entered the small room the cloak had vanished, but a couple of days later a clairvoyant medium saw a phantom of a priest bending over the piscina.

In June 1974 the clairvoyant returned to find water in the holy bowl and the caretaker was affected by the feeling of 'an unhappy presence' on the spiral staircase.

A former labourer on the adjoining farm stated that the chapel 'in his day', over sixty years ago, was used for storing hay and straw and he found an old corn mill in the room. Because of the value of the produce he often used to sleep in the room beneath and frequently heard the sound of footsteps pacing the floor overhead. 'It was always in June,' he said. 'I don't know why.'

Do we now?

CHAPTER 5

THE VILLAGE AND CASTLE OF CHILHAM

An unexpected arrival into Chilham village can be a little bewildering, for one gets the feeling of having been transported into another century. No modern encumbrances such as parking meters or street lamps dispel the atmosphere of a medieval age. The only symbols, at first glance, of the twentieth century are a discreet sign directing motorists to the 'Free Car Park' and hardly discernible white lines in the village square.

We had arrived in the fifteenth-century village one pleasant sunny day to learn more about the phantoms of the castle, but had been initially delayed by the attractive beauty of the surroundings. It is one of the twelve loveliest villages in England and must have gained a top position in the league, yet it is only minutes away from the M20 motorway, although thankfully out of earshot of it.

Adjoining the entrance to the ancient flint-walled Church of St Mary, which has a sarcophagus purporting to have contained the remains of St Augustine, is the fifteenth-century *White Horse Inn.* Besides the normal liquid refreshment, this building offers an additional attraction—the possibility of meeting the ghost of a former owner and vicar of Chilham, the Reverend Sampson Hieron.

In the seventeenth century the building had been the vicarage, but the incumbent had proved 'difficult': he was a non-conformist and was evicted because of his attitude. His ghost, that of a grey-haired old gentleman wearing a gown and gaiters, has, it is said, been seen in the mornings standing in a 'typical pose' warming himself in front of the inglenook fire. The fireplace itself is of the fifteenth century, the lintel with its carved roses only being exposed during renovations in 1956.

A more macabre incident was the discovery under the kitchen floor of two male skeletons, which may well be connected with the nearby churchyard or the horrific stories linked with the castle keep.

Down a side road one finds excellent examples of old timbered Wealden houses and also a half-timbered house, the former vicarage of Ezekias Fogg, now an art gallery known as Robins Croft. It is claimed that from the side of this truly magnificent example of Tudor architecture an unknown phantom used to appear and on its arrival a ghostly horse, which silently gallops from the churchyard down towards the house, stops and returns to its 'home' among the graves.

Chilham itself owes its foundation to the Romans, but possibly Neolithic man walked nearby for an ancient path runs through the parish near the top of the Downs. This route has become known locally as the Pilgrim's Way, but starts at Winchester and is therefore merely an off-shoot from the path of Chaucer's pilgrims.

The castle, built on Roman and Saxon foundations, was constructed by Bishop Odo, half-brother of William the Conqueror, but was rebuilt in 1616 by Sir Dudley Digges. The estate had been granted to Sir Thomas Cheyney by Henry VIII in 1542, but when he moved, much of the structure of the castle was removed to create his new home in the Isle of Sheppey.

It is now the private home of the Viscount Massereene and Ferrard who opens the grounds and deer park, housing one of the oldest heronries in Britain, to the public during the summer season. Displays of free-flying eagles and falcons are also offered as an added attraction.

The only part of the original Norman castle, built in

1068, that remains is the octagonal keep which has walls 8ft thick in places.

We were rather dramatically introduced to the castle by the twenty-one-year-old son of the tenant, Charles Jardine, who led us in complete darkness down old worn stone steps into one of the dungeons. Here in the flickering candlelight I saw skin-covered benches round the walls, chain mail and rusting chains hanging from the stones and, dominating the room, a bar offering a wide range of drinks to the visitor.

Charles told us that in this eerie darkened room, some 20ft in diameter, 800 prisoners were kept in worse conditions than those of the Black Hole of Calcutta. Many of them manacled to the walls, the half-starved men would become mere animals until the victors decided to rid themselves of their commitments.

Pointing to a steeply angled window the young guide explained that it led to a well which provided the means of disposal. The prisoners would be unable to get out, the aperture was too narrow, but above us, amid the decorations on the ceiling, was a 'plug' which would be opened and gallons of water, pumped up from the well, would cascade into the writhing mass of half-humans below.

In the floor was another aperture to ensure that those beneath, for there was another dungeon deeper in the earth, be drowned first. The water would then seep eventually into the chalk subsoil and back into the well for re-use. 'The bodies,' he said, 'would then be thrown to the wolves.'

Confirming some of this horrific picture workmen digging a few years ago in one of the dungeons, probably the lower one, found six male skeletons, one of which was still bound to the mould covered walls by a rusty chain.

Charles told us that he and his father were probably the first to enter this part of the castle for 'about 200 years' when they took it over about five years ago. 'We found a skeleton of a roe deer on the floor and they have been extinct in this region since the seventeenth century.' The Dungeon Bar is one of the attractions for groups of tourists and visitors who enjoy the regular medieval banquets held in the keep every Friday and Saturday evening.

Of the ghost we were told that it is of a 'medieval lady'. It seems that a couple of years ago one of the young ladies acting as a 'serving wench' saw the figure of another woman in medieval clothing outside near the old wall and gateway. Assuming it was a guest she greeted the lady, who just melted into the wall beside the gateway, frightening the waitress so much she ran in to the bar still white and shaking and demanding a brandy. She had never drunk anything before, we were assured, 'and she was certainly scared out of her wits'.

Earlier in 1974 an actress in a television film being made in the castle grounds was pushed by unseen hands down the stairway towards the dungeon. Her leg was hurt and had to be bandaged.

We were guided back up to ground level and into another room, the main banqueting area, and then into the kitchen. It was in here that mysterious tapping has been heard coming from behind the wall. By looking at the design and layout of the walls it can be seen that their apparent thickness at this point is some 10–12ft which leads one to suspect the presence of a sealed room. The outlines of an old archway and a doorway are just visible in the main room, and above it the prominence of a sealed fireplace that is still in existence in an upper room. I wondered what could possibly be behind those dark dust-covered stones and shivered, for I had been told of a 'lady friend' of one of the owners in the fourteenth century having been bricked up somewhere in the tower; it is said that she haunted the ancient walls in Victorian days.

We reached the Lucius Room, named after the first Christian King of the Britons and thought to be the original founder of the castle. It was in here that an earthenware vase was seen to move from the window sill until it reached the centre of the room where 'it just dropped and smashed'. The witnesses, Charles Jardine and a friend, had stood amazed in the doorway which was about 8ft from the window. 'We just didn't know what to think or do.'

In the Regency Room two years ago, one of the large windows though locked and bolted in five places, suddenly blew open when Mr Jardine was standing at the other side of the room. This room, the main sitting-room of a former rather ecentric owner, was decorated in typical Regency style even to a 'gold-leafed ceiling'. I gathered that the previous occupier gambled away his entire estate and his wife.

The most haunted room in the keep is, perhaps surprisingly in view of the appalling mass murders committed in the dungeons, the ladies' powder room. It was certainly at the time of our visit the coldest room in the castle.

It was here that Charles Jardine frequently heard a woman humming and the sounds from above of furniture being moved around but there is nothing above other than the roof of the keep. From there we enjoyed a marvellous view of the surrounding countryside and noticed that apart from a weather vane and a water tank there was nothing that would account for the noises that the guide had heard.

An Alsatian dog brought to the doorway of that room had refused to enter, howled and rushed downstairs.

Outside again in the cheerful sunshine we looked at the tall, grim building, holding its secrets of mass murder and the identity of a medieval lady. We walked to the side of the tower to examine the old donkey-operated wellhead. Most of the mechanism and wooden cogged wheel used to pump up the water still remains in situ, and efforts will be made to completely restore it to full working order, but not to use in drowning customers we were assured.

Boxley Hotel, Kent.

The haunted 'corridor' of the Seven Stars, Robertsbridge, Sussex. At the far end a steep narrow stairway leads to the loft and the mysterious 70 ft. deep shaft.

Blackboys Inn, Cross in Hand, Nr. Heathfield, Sussex.

Eyhorne Manor. The 'haunted' bedroom.

Michelham Priory.

The Old Soar Chapel, Plaxtol, Kent. Phantom footsteps are heard and a ghostly cloak was seen once in an upstairs room.

Puttenden Manor, Nr. Lingfield, Surrey.

The sitting room of the former home of the author, 'haunted' by the smell of tobacco.

Barn Cottages, Hayes Lane, Kenley, Surrey. The phantom 'grey lady' has been seen in the back garden of these cottages.

The Keep of Chilham Castle.

Pashley Manor, Nr. Ticehurst, Kent.

George Hotel, Robertsbridge, Sussex.

Eyhorne Manor, Hollingbourne, Nr. Maidstone, Kent.

Boys Hall, Willesborough, Nr. Ashford, Kent.

The hallway, Boys Hall, Willesborough, Kent.

The haunted bedroom of Boys Hall, Willesborough, Nr. Ashford, Kent.

CHAPTER 6

THE BOXLEY HOTEL

Arthur Mee in his Kent volume of *The Kings' England* describes the village of Boxley as 'the land of pure delight . . . a beautiful corner of England'. That was some forty years ago and development has altered the countryside by placing a large residential estate of 'ticky-tacky boxes' on the outskirts of this 'beautiful corner'. Nevertheless the village centre itself remains untouched and unharmed, and retains the charm which attracted and inspired Tennyson to produce many of his works.

Cecilia Tennyson, sister of the poet, had joined Edmund Lushington at Sandling Park and to be near the lovers Tennyson had moved into Boxley Park. Surrounded as it is by undulating carpets of green fields and hills, and with a tiny stream running through the grounds to join the River Medway near Allington Castle, we can see from where Tennyson received his inspiration. Parts of 'The Prologue to the Princess' but more especially 'The Brook' can obviously be linked to the poet's life in this part of Kent.

The attractive little church itself contains an unusual monument recording the gratitude of Sir Henry Wyatt to a cat for saving his life. When imprisoned in the Tower of London in 1483, the furry animal would sleep on his chest at night keeping him warm and during the day would provide him with food in the shape of pigeons. Other notable tombs are those of George Sandys, the Lushingtons and, of course, Cecilia Tennyson.

Modified from a Norman cloister, the porch displays an ancient carving believed to portray Edward II, a visitor to the village in 1321, but the history of Boxley is older than this.

The manor once belonged, like Chilham Castle, to Odo, the Bishop of Bayeux, and in 1189 Richard I presented the estate to the Cistercian Order who built an abbey there. This building was once one of the most famous of its type in Norman England, but all that is left is a house containing stones from it and a rebuilt barn. Emphasising the status of the abbey it was one of the abbots from here who conducted the service over Thomas à Becket in Canterbury.

Following the Reformation, Sir Thomas Wyatt of Allington Castle became the owner of the estate, but with the downfall of the family when he was executed for treason, the family forfeited the manor, although part of it was returned to them when Elizabeth came to the throne.

One of the old buildings of the estate was believed to have been occupied at one time by Thomas Vicary, founder of the Royal College of Surgeons in 1460. This house was known as Boxley House.

In the seventeenth century Edwin Wyatt, who had successfully sued Lady Selyard for part of the manor, demolished all but a minor section of the building and reconstructed it.

Some time later Lord Romney, who had inherited the house, sold it to Sir John Styles, a well-known brewer who carried out a certain amount of modernisation to the interior. The Styles family were to occupy Boxley for over 100 years and it was during their ownership that a tragic incident occurred which was recalled with frightening clarity in the 1960s.

In 1953 a barrister, Mr Marr Johnson, purchased the house and remained there until the current owner Mr T. J. Knowlden bought it late in 1964. Under his direction the house became initially a country club and then, as now, a popular hotel. It remains essentially a seventeenth-century house with Georgian additions.

Shortly after the Knowldens purchased the building they

were given a copy of a report taken from a local paper, believed to be that of the *Maidstone Gazette,* relating to a burglary and a suicide, but it was only in 1965 that the relevance of this cutting became apparent.

One afternoon about 3.30 pm Mrs Knowlden and her mother were standing outside the house near the front door discussing the plans for the future. Builders were still decorating the house in preparation for its opening as a club.

Mrs Knowlden glanced towards the lounge and bar. Through the window she saw a stranger in the lounge and drew her mother's attention to him by asking 'Who is that?'

Both the ladies watched as the figure glided from beside the bar and through the reception lounge towards the counter and stairway. Describing the apparition later, the owner's wife said that 'he was a short man with black hair brushed well back and was wearing a cut away coat. We both saw him quite clearly and because he looked like some sort of butler we wondered who on earth he could be'.

The newspaper report was suddenly recalled and found. Dated July 1898 it was headed 'A Butler's Shocking Suicide. Strange Sequel to a Burglary'. The report continued, 'Great consternation was caused in the village of Boxley on Tuesday morning when it became known that Thomas Sales, the butler at Boxley House, the residence of Miss Style, had committed suicide by shooting himself in the pantry.'

Thomas had been employed in the house for some twenty years and had in that time gained a good reputation among the local villagers. But on the previous Thursday a burglary had occurred and although of 'a very extensive character', nothing was stolen except for 'two rugs against the front door which was unlocked'.

The police were puzzled, for not only were they unable to find where the burglars broke in, ignoring the unlocked front door, but any clue which would lead them to the criminals.

Up to the alleged burglary Thomas Sales had been a cheerful character but his attitude changed with the arrival of the police, as it would do. His wife, however, commented on the difference in her husband when she left him, presumably to return home, on the Sunday evening. 'He seemed to have something troubling him,' she said, 'but would give no indication as to the cause of his worry.'

The newspaper report states that 'the deceased had referred but slightly to the late robbery only remarking that it was a very mysterious affair'. His concern, however, had deepened so much that he was unable to sleep at all that night, though in the morning he appeared more cheerful.

Breakfast was served to him in his pantry by the cook, but when she came to collect the plates she found the door locked and a smell of gunpowder near the door. She looked through the window and, seeing Thomas sitting rigidly in his chair, became alarmed and called the police.

They broke down the door and discovered the butler had 'shattered his head with a gun'.

On questioning other servants it was learnt that the butler was convinced the police were suspicious of him and felt that he was about to be arrested for the crime. This was not true, but papers found on him claimed that the burglary was committed by seven men who had threatened to kill him if he informed on them.

It is unusual to find so easily the identity and dating of a phantom, but there can be little doubt as to who that mysterious man was who glided through the reception hall that summer evening.

To increase toilet facilities for male customers it had been decided to convert the butler's pantry into a lavatory and to create an entrance in the lounge. Surely the easiest place to have a doorway would be where there was an original door? But in carrying out the work it seems that the atmosphere of that half-forgotten disaster has been released, for the ghostly butler has made his presence known on more than one occasion.

When two ladies were coming down the stairs to the reception area they were suddenly pushed from behind by unseen hands. Thankfully they were able to save themselves from stumbling and getting hurt. A gentleman customer had also had the same experience.

Mrs Cornford, a friend of the Knowldens, told me that early morning staff had also seen the figure of the butler gliding from the 'gentlemens' towards the stairway, but he vanishes at the archway in the lounge.

The building retains the atmosphere of the Georgian period for its modern facilties and décor have been successfully blended in without disturbing the comfort of those earlier days.

One reminder of that affluent age still remains, although no doubt in time he will fade and become just another mention in the papers of Boxley's history.

CHAPTER 7

MICHELHAM PRIORY, UPPER DICKER

'. . . here in this double moated Peace, where Faith allied to Beauty gives Release, Men found and still find ease of heart and soul . . .' are the words of Canon Greville Cooke and give some indication of the tranquility and beauty of the ancient priory of Michelham.

The first building that visitors see is the Mill House standing on the edge of the huge seven-acre moat which itself encloses a further plot of the same size. The moat is believed to be of Norman origin though the site is that of a Saxon manor house, named Michelham because the river Cuckmere curves at this point, and is described by the Saxon phrase *michel hamm,* meaning 'large bend'.

Once on the outskirts of the extensive Ashdown forest, evidence of which remains in several massive oak trees, the priory was founded in 1229 for a group of Augustinian canons by Gilbert de Aquila III who, having selected the island as the ideal situation, found it necessary to demolish a Norman building before starting work on what was to become a 'double moated Peace'.

Legend has it that Thomas à Becket's first miracle was performed near the Mill House. Richard de Aquila, grand-father of the founder, had been taking Thomas hunting, but when crossing a mill stream the young man, together with his horse, fell and it was only thanks to the miraculous closing of the sluice gates that the future archbishop of Canterbury was saved from a painful death beneath the mill wheel.

The early history of Michelham is a mixture of strife and happiness, witchcraft and devout worship.

Only six years after work commenced, Gilbert de Aquila returned home to L'Aigle in Normandy, leaving the priory only half finished. King Henry III, having granted the the Licence for the foundation, was justifiably annoyed and demanded the return of the lands which included eighty acres at Michelham, the wood at Pevensey and pasture in 'Brul and Diker'.

The first prior was a man named Roger who was, it seems, to control the site for only ten years before Peter succeeded him in 1239, under the Bishops of Chichester, who were superiors of the priory until 1536. The work must have proceeded slowly and painfully, creating a disturbing effect on the community.

Priors came and went after spending only a few years there and in 1348 the scourge of the Black Death caused many casualties amongst the community, reducing the number of canons to a mere five. It took five years to regain the figure of thirteen.

Between 1283, when Prior Nicholas was fined for un-authorised absence, and the Peasants' Revolt of 1381, life in the house of religion was far from tranquil. One prior went to Rome because of a dispute over Hailsham Church and the monks of Bayham were ejected as a result on two occasions; four trespassers imprisoned within its walls for three years were compulsorily released and in 1313 a poacher, William de Marle, was granted a pardon for services to Edward I, only after serving many months incarcerated within the priory's walls.

However, in 1376 the appointment of yet another prior, John Leame or Leem, proved to be a pleasing highlight in the sorrowful history of the Order. One of his first actions was to enlarge the small gatehouse as a precaution against the angry peasants who were demonstrating against the vicious poll-tax.

Because of John's enthusiasm, energy and his organising ability, he had formed a small force of local villagers to counter the devastating attacks by French raiders and increased the funds of the priory appreciably. He also achieved considerable loyalty and popularity among his colleagues. Later records confirm that John was considered as an extremely kind and considerate man, even though he collected rent for John of Gaunt.

Leame must have become absolutely devoted to Michelham, like so many other people through the ages up to, and including, the present day. From a description given by a possible witness, he was tall and good looking with 'friendly eyes, full of kindness' expressing the love for his community of brothers and his fellow men.

It is particularly unfortunate that this truly honourable man was unable to influence his successors, for although in the forty years of his administration he had succeeded in bringing to Michelham no small measure of contentment, his work was quite undone by later priors who caused a complete disruption of the atmosphere and organisation.

They were careless and incompetent, allowing the building to fall into disrepair and the food stocks to diminish with appalling results. William Landon, after only three years, was removed with ignominy in 1438, and in the following nine years under Laurence Wynchelse the magnificent seal of the priory was lost and financial support from various sources was curtailed. The dispirited friars, hungry and miserable, were often to be found in local hostelries cavorting in a a most unseemly fashion.

The situation had deteriorated to such an extent that in 1441 it had become necessary to order the prior to pay the priests 'four nobles and the Canons twenty shillings per annum' for their upkeep and to get the main storage barn and kitchen repaired. Hardly an enviable life for the inmates, as in those days a noble was the equivalent of 34p.

The last prior was Thomas Holbeme who, on the Dissolution in 1536, received a pension of £20 from King Henry, but only after Cromwell's agents had stripped the lead from the roof of the buildings, stolen the five magnificent bells and demolished most of the main construction of the priory, leaving only the refectory and the western wing as reminders of happier days of Michelham.

When the estate was divided amongst the King's friends, including Anne of Cleves, the ruins remained unaltered for some forty years until the Pelham family, attracted by the position and the charm of the area, purchased the site from the Crown.

The Pelhams, whose forefathers had arrived with William the Conqueror, were obviously anxious to restore the ruins to a habitable state and added a magnificent farmhouse to the priory walls. They also re-roofed the refectory, changing its use from a dining-room to a kitchen and a storage shed. Other rebuilding with stones from the original house produced a comfortable private house, the first ever on the site.

However, because, as in so many cases today, the owners had failed to realise the cost of renovation and general maintenance, the Pelhams, after only fifteen years' occupation, were forced to sell up and move on.

The new owners, the Sackvilles, although retaining Michelham for nearly three hundred years, also found costs high and leased the property to the Child family from 1791 to 1861. By the early 1800s the Childs had sub-let the property to local farmers one of whom became, like so many predecessors devoted to Michelham, anxious to buy it for himself, but whilst in the course of negotiation the Sackvilles sold it to Mr J. E. A. Gwynne of Folkington, pronounced as 'Fowington' by the locals.

The farmer was furious that what he had hoped would be his home had been 'sold over his head' and not even to another Sussex family, but to a Midlander known as 'The Iron Master', who only wanted the ground for shooting over. When the new owner arrived somewhat conceitedly mounted on a white stallion 'like some massive war horse' prepared, one imagines, to do battle with the local peasantry, the tenant farmer must have let his feelings be known in no uncertain terms. Although nobody knows exactly what happened when Mr Gwynne and the farmer met, the horse returned to Folkington Place riderless. Gwynne eventually arrived home but 'in a rage the like of which we had never experienced before'.

It is pure coincidence that the Gwynne family are associated with two haunted properties in the county, one at Polegate and here at Michelham. They continued with the massive task of restoring the priory adding a top floor and roof to the west wing, but in 1923 they too decided to find a new owner of the ancient site and sold the property to Mr Beresford-Wright.

Whether any phenomena had ever occurred before this period is not known, but it was during the Wrights' occupation that some of the phantoms that inhabit Michelham were first reported. A disastrous fire in 1927 burnt out the Tudor farmhouse and for days afterwards, whilst still recovering from the shock, Mr Beresford-Wright found his horses in their stables shaking with abject terror and covered with sweat. He was puzzled and a little alarmed at the state of the animals.

Weeks later the creatures were heard kicking their stable walls and the owner, running to ascertain the cause, found the horses 'extremely disturbed and were obviously badly scared'. A stable boy, on being questioned, was equally puzzled by the state of his charges, but suggested that the cause of the fright may have been created by the 'huge white stallion which keeps on coming in from somewhere'.

Another mystery reported by the Wrights was that several friends claimed that they were met at the gatehouse by a 'charming gentleman who smiled and pointed to where the house lay as if directing us'. Descriptions of the figure, who although 'a pleasant character' remained silent, matched those of an Augustinian prior. His hair was cut to resemble Christ's crown of thorns and he wore a dark cloak and a white 'under-skirt' with open sandals.

One or two of the visitors, on turning round after thanking their 'guide', were puzzled to find that the figure had disap-peared. 'He must have moved very quickly.' The owners of the priory were more than a little puzzled for they had no knowledge of 'the monk'. There is a strong belief and a certain amount of evidence that the apparition, if that is what was seen, was that of the popular John Leame who must have loved Michelham with all his heart and soul. He would be only too delighted to welcome new friends and visitors to the community which had provided him and his colleagues with so much happiness.

Another phantom also made its first appearance at about the same time.

One evening a couple of friends of the Beresford-Wrights, strolling through the grounds on a pleasant summer evening, saw a figure of a woman dressed in a grey gown standing on the bridge in front of the gatehouse and looking sorrow-fully into the moat beneath. On enquiring as to the identity of 'the other guest' the couple were told, with curiosity, that they were the only people staying at Michelham that week-end. The incident was partly forgotten until other reports were received a few months later that the woman had been seen on numerous occasions by several other people visiting the priory.

Mr Beresford-Wright, determined to identify the myster-ious woman, was unable to arrive at any conclusion from his enquiries, except that there was a possibility the wraith could have been that of a member of the Sackville family whose young daughter fell into the water and drowned.

In 1951 ownership of Michelham was transferred to Mr F. G. H. Storey and then in 1959 a relative of the Storey family, Mrs R. H. Hotblack née Skrine, donated the priory to the Sussex Archaeological Trust.

Due to the intense archaeological interest in the building, the ruins and the overall site, considerable excavation plans were carried out and continue to provide an increasing amount of information concerning life and its problems in the earlier years.

It was only in 1970 that workers unexpectedly discovered foundations of a wall and a hearth in the lawns on the edge of the moat. Diggers, under the supervision of the new owners, have exposed the foundations of a large hall constructed in the thirteenth century. Unfortunately due to the conditions, the site being continually filled with water from the moat lying as it does well below the water level, it will not be long before the ancient remains are permanently covered over.

It has been established that later additions to the original construction possibly changed its use to a workshop and then, because of the water level of the adjoining moat rising alarmingly, a new floor was laid and ovens were added probably in the sixteenth century.

One of the most recent exciting finds, however, was only discovered when laying new drains to the priory itself in 1972. A small group of workmen, instructed to use only spades and forks because of the possibility of damaging valuable remains, were carefully digging a trench when suddenly one of them saw the top of an old jar sticking out of the soil near the outer wall. The object was gently eased out of the earth and found to be a perfect specimen of a Bellarmini jar containing a large number of badly rusted pins stuck into a round blackened lump of unidentified substance.

Bellarmine jars, or jugs, were made with the image of Bishop Bellarmine on one side as a derogatory feature aimed at lampooning the reverend gentleman or, as some believe, using 'sympathetic magic' to harm the bishop. The cause of this unsavoury attitude was that he had been very outspoken against witches and sorcery during the medieval times when the practising of a bit of magic was very popular in Europe.

To add to the revenge of the annoyed populace many of

the jugs were used as containers for 'spells' and 'witches brews' to such an extent that they became known as 'witch jars'.

The objects from the 1972 find and the jar itself are now displayed in the priory, having been returned after a full examination by the British Museum. The discovery of such an object in a spot adjoining a religious house of this nature can only suggest that witchcraft was actively pursued here in the medieval period and it is perhaps a survivor of a day when one of the canons, perhaps John Leame himself, preached against 'the vileness of such devil worship'. It would be natural for a local witch to cast a spell or even a curse on the prior, or even on the whole building, in evil revenge and then bury the pot containing the heart of a sheep or a goat, or worse still a newborn child, punctured with pins, as close to the walls as possible. This would ensure that the strength of the curse was concentrated on that particular part of the house which was once used as the priors' rooms.

Just after lunch on a glorious summer day in 1972 a woman in a grey gown approached the ticket kiosk in the gatehouse. 'She was thin and looked very ill', said the attendant, 'and then I realised she had a small black and white dog with her. I told her that dogs were not permitted, but she just seemed to glide past a couple of other visitors waiting for tickets and I was unable to stop her. I wasn't all that worried for I knew she would be asked to leave as soon as she was seen by one of the guides, but there was certainly something peculiar about her'.

The other visitors, a middle-aged couple, took their tickets and passed through the gateway. The woman turned to her husband and commented on the unusual dress worn by the woman in front of them, the woman with the black and white dog who had 'so rudely' passed them without paying. Her companion was puzzled and asked what woman she was talking about. He apparently was completely unable to see the figure. His wife, realising this, began to get a little annoyed and at that moment, to the consternation of the visitor and the attendant in the kiosk, both the female apparition and that of the dog 'just faded away'.

It is not difficult to hazard a guess as to the identity of that silent, white-faced visitor. It is not difficult to imagine the sorrowing distress of the mother who haunts the gatehouse, pitifully, sadly, unable to accept the death of her baby daughter who had slipped so easily from her arms that fateful day some three hundred years previously. Drawn forever to the spot of that heartrending tragedy and seen perhaps mainly by other mothers who must at some time during their lives have shared a similar appalling fright, but without, one hopes, such tragic results. The figure was seen once or twice between 1969 and 1972, but never with such clarity as on that occasion.

Only a few weeks later in the main hall of the Tudor house, completely rebuilt after the terrible fire nearly fifty years ago, occurred one of the biggest mysteries in the history of the priory.

A young couple were reading an explanatory notice fitted on one of the walls and turned round to relate the details with the objects in the room behind them. What they saw stunned them. Descending from the ceiling in a diagonal direction was the figure of a middle-aged man, 'rather handsomely dressed and wearing a cloak'. As he neared the floor in front of the inglenook fireplace he jumped without a sound as if from an invisible step and glided silently but very quickly through the end doorway.

The young visitors looked at each other in absolute amazement, unable to believe their eyes, unable to accept that other people in the room had failed to see the weird arrival and departure of the strange apparition. However, before they had time to move, another figure, that of a middle-aged woman 'in a Tudor gown', suddenly rushed out of the farthest room at the western end and hurried past them as if in silent pursuit of the now vanished man.

Intensive investigations followed. The questions arose but

no answers could be provided. Had there been a staircase where the fireplace now stands? Who was the man? Who was chasing him and why? The custodian admitted that the room had been rebuilt without any record of an original staircase being in existence. 'But', he pointed out, 'that was a long time ago. There is no logical reason that there should not have been a staircase there, probably an external one, and thus the woman might have originally been in the garden'.

There have been so many alterations since the fire in 1927, but there are most certainly signs of one staircase on the outer wall of the buttery and there is no reason to suppose that there might not have been another.

The latest phenomena reported at the priory was of mysterious bells being heard by Mr and Mrs Lett, the resident caretakers, when walking up the main staircase one evening in 1974. 'I couldn't understand it', Mrs Lett said, 'there are only two bells here and neither was ringing at the time. One of them couldn't anyway as it was tied up. The evening was rather sultry, not a breath of wind, just quiet and peaceful'.

'Quiet and peaceful'; the atmosphere of Michelham remains undisturbed. Regardless of the sorrow suffered within its ancient walls, despite the intense anger directed at a stranger and the probable curse set by some old and wrinkled crone, the ghosts have never frightened anyone. They merge into the natural tranquility of the priory as mist in an evening dusk. Michelham continues to offer to all men 'ease of heart and soul'.

CHAPTER 8

BLACKBOYS, HEATHFIELD

Travelling home late one stormy night from a radio interview at Brighton, I fancied a drink and, nearing Heathfield, pulled into the forecourt of the *Blackboys Inn*. With the wind howling round the ancient eaves and rain lashing itself into a fury, it was not the sort of night that brought forth even regular customers. There was only one car parked on the gravel and, as I hurried into the warmth and welcome of the saloon, I was not really surprised to find only one other customer in the bar.

Whilst quietly swigging my lager, the initial and natural apprehensive attitude concerning the arrival of a stranger slowly faded and the barman, a young man in his early thirties, asked me if I was interested in ghosts. To strengthen my assurance that I was not only interested but somewhat knowledgeable on the subject I showed him a copy of my book, *Our Haunted Kingdom*.

With that the other customer, a man in his mid-twenties, jumped off his stool and asked to see the book. Peter, the barman, called to his wife who, white and shaking, was obviously suffering from shock.

The girl nervously fingered a teacloth and told me of the experience that had frightened them both the previous night.

'We were just clearing up after closing', she said, 'when we heard footsteps overhead. Peter ran up the stairs to find out who it was, but came back a bit shaken. We knew the only people in the house were us, but there was just a possibility of a stray customer still being here. But there was nobody about. The place was empty.

'Shortly afterwards, when in the end lounge, I suddenly felt very cold and heard the floorboards creak just as if someone walked on them. I was scared and I don't think Peter was very happy either. I am sure it was Anne.'

The woman mentioned was the daughter of a former licensee of the establishment and now lies buried in Framfield churchyard.

Anne was born in 1765 of Mr and Mrs Thomas Starr and, although little is known about her parents, it can safely be assumed that the father was not new to the licensed trade. *Blackboys Inn* was orginally constructed in 1389 as a farmhouse but, as agriculture in the area slowly deteriorated, the farmland was sold for building purposes. Even in those early days there was a shortage of houses for the growing population of Sussex.

The building, still rather remote and set back from the main road, but within easy reach of the nearby village of Cross in Hand, was an ideal situation for a pub. And so in the early eighteenth century the doors were opened to the public and the delights of the hop offered to all and sundry.

The new facilities attracted immediate attention from the locals, the shopkeepers, the workers still employed on farms and the hop-pickers. Everyone had to come and try out the ale. It was good and the reputation of *Blackboys Inn* spread. Soon travellers from Lewes to Heathfield and beyond began to call in to sample the beer and the hospitality.

The trade increased beyond all original hopes and the Starrs rapidly found it impossible to cope with the growing number of 'regulars'.

The profits being made would ably cover the costs of an addition to the living-in permanent staff and so it was that a cousin was asked to join them.

By then Anne was 38 and, to the distress of her mother, still unwed. She was not an ugly woman, but just rather plain in features. Thomas, her father, having brought her up in the environment of a pub, realised that she was no great catch, but would have been distressed to see her leave to get married. 'She could live with her husband here', he had frequently pointed out to his wife when discussing the future of their only child.

What of the feelings of the woman herself? Knowing nothing other than hard strenuous work behind the bar, the daily cleaning, the early and late hours, the troubles with the drunks, she must have often suffered many pangs of frustration and envy when alone at night. Would she never be a wife and a mother? Never know the delights of having a child of her own and a husband to take her away from the constant smell of the beers and pipe tobacco?

Then one day William, her cousin, arrived. A strong sturdy character, 'ideal for cellar work' was her father's comment, and good-looking in a rough sort of way. He was a man who enjoyed the company of women—all women. The lady travellers accompanied by their gentlemen and the farmers' wives coming in for a quick tot of gin were all one to him. His quick humour, his strong character and roguish looks caused many a flutter of heart-strings whenever he ventured into Heathfield. It was also thought that much of the increased trade was due to his arrival, for he was just as popular with the men.

He was well-known in the market and would often be seen arguing in a humorous mood about the price of a joint for the family's Sunday lunch, or playfully flirting with one of the girls of the village.

Tongues began to work overtime. Was he married? Had he left some poor wife somewhere pining over her loss? Did he plan on settling down? What were his feelings about his cousin Anne?

Late one night William and the Starrs were talking in the lounge. The large room at the end of the building had recently been opened to accommodate a greater number of customers and to provide a place where the locals could chat about market prices, play darts or the occasional game of bar billiards away from the gentlefolks' idle chatter. Few locals were interested in the activities of the town unless some exciting crime was being heard in the Court at Lewes, whilst the visitors were more concerned with the latest fashions, the activities of the politicians or the current attitude of the Church.

This particular day had been a tiring one. Right up to closing time the pub had been crowded. A large sale at the market had brought in dozens of thirsty travellers, potential buyers, curious villagers and the usual smattering of rogues and vagabonds from the surrounding hamlets. The family had been on their feet for hours, bustling here and there with the orders whilst William had been up and down the cellar stairs dealing with the barrels and crates 'like a blasted slave'.

The exhausted group chatted over their frothing beer in the welcoming quietness, discussing the day's toils, quirks of individual customers and the general gossip of the day. The older pair, Thomas and his wife, began to show their tiredness and, emptying their mugs, bid the younger couple 'good-night' and wearily climbed the ancient stairs.

William was now able to really study Anne for the first time. She was vivacious, had a shapely figure and, although nearing middle age, not bad looking: 'quite a comely lass, really'.

Anne, realising that her cousin was assessing her, laughed but her thoughts too ran on similar lines. William was a flirt, but he was a man, a handsome man and a worker. She had noticed several young girls making eyes at him when they had been in the village together. True, he was not the sort of mate she would have chosen, but time was passing and as her thoughts developed and her cousin refilled her mug she began to feel a familiar urge within her body. A tingling sensation began to affect her. She grew bolder, more forward.

William, whose mind was beginning to haze, found it increasingly difficult to focus his eyes on the woman in front of him. He bent over to her holding his hand out.

'Let's go to bed, Anne. It's getting late.'

75

The morning found them lying snuggled together in the four-poster bed in the main room over the bar.

Months passed. The Starrs accepted the situation and hoped it would resolve itself. Comments were often made of marriage and the fact that the village was talking. William continued to discuss the problem with vague promises. Anne meanwhile, whilst suffering pangs of conscience, was also getting increasingly worried as time went by.

Eventually it became obvious that Anne Starr was pregnant and it was with mixed feelings she continued on in her work. At last she was to experience the joy of motherhood, but not as a wife. Would William ever agree to marriage?

They all knew finances were tight. A pub could only make so much profit and another mouth to feed would seriously stretch resources. William promised to see about getting another job and, in his searches for a new position, had to be away from the pub for long periods. Suspicion mounted. 'Surely he could get work in the village which would provide more money? Surely he didn't have to go as far away as Lewes to get a better job?' He didn't, but it was 1840 and George IV had set the pace for good living.

William's absences grew more frequent and of longer periods until the day arrived for Anne to give birth. Strong she may have been but, with William away, more work had fallen on to her shoulders and the tempo of the pub's business could not allow for rest for anyone.

She finally collapsed and was carried to bed. Searing pain tore at her body. Her mother, fraught with anxiety, with duty to her husband and to the business, was unable to deal with her daughter. During hours of silent torment Anne suffered alone, alone in the bedroom where William had told her of his love, had proved so passionate that her fulfilment as a woman was now only moments away. She heard the sounds in the room below. The customers laughing and joking, and as closing time approached the farewells and ribald comments before they departed. She dare not scream.

She had to be quiet. She tore the sheets in her agony, her lips bleeding from clenching her teeth with the pain.

The doors finally slammed shut on the last regular. Mrs Starr ran to her daughter lying in that solitary silent room. For a second she saw the now peaceful figure of Anne lying twisted in her last spasm stretched across the bed—a tortured creature who had finally succumbed to the racking, searing anguish of a still-birth.

Without a sound the mother collapsed unconscious to the floor. She never fully recovered from the nagging sense of guilt at the desertion of her daughter when she was needed most. It was not long before she and her husband were seen no longer at Blackboys.

Of the whereabouts and eventual departure of William we know nothing, but is it he who walks unseen through that lounge in the late hours recalling again the thoughts of passion which had been roused, the passion which finally killed his mistress and child?

Anne, poor Anne, can still be heard pacing the bedroom floor and opening the doors overcome with anxiety, with worry, with conscience and yet still with love for the man who in his heartlessness deserted her when her soul cried out for him.

Walking round the inn today, ducking beneath the ancient, darkened beams, up narrow twisting stairways, over aged floors which slope in all directions one feels that someone watches. A pathetic, pitiful someone who so much desired motherhood and yet in her last moments on this earth was to be cheated of that ultimate happiness.

Yet also there is mystery. Compare the thickness of walls in one of the upper rooms and one finds a discrepancy of some eighteen inches. Does this unaccountable bulge contain what legend claims is a sealed alcove? Does it contain some hidden loot cached there by one of the robbers of the road who frequented the area like night-riding hawks? One day perhaps an answer will be provided.

As the barman and I returned after examining those corridors and rooms of suffering, I found my other temporary companion in the 'new lounge'—the room in which it has been presumed William and Anne realised their feelings for each other. It was cold and creaky, but as the rain continued to beat against the walls I told myself the noises were of dry timbers protesting against the heavy buffeting of the raging elements outside.

The other customer, chatting with the barman's wife, looked up and asked about my thoughts concerning Anne, and as we continued discussing the phenomena I learnt that the door to the adjoining room leading out on to the forecourt had been found inexplicably unlatched and open on more than one occasion. Would this have been the doorway which William used the last time he went to Lewes never to return?

'Why not come and see our cottage?' enquired the customer. 'We have another real ghost there.'

The following month saw me driving along a twisting lane about a mile south of the inn. The drive led me to the charming country home of a very well-known actor. After a very friendly welcome he asked me not to mention his name. 'It would prove embarrassing.' I assured him he would remain anonymous as far as any report of mine was concerned and, relieved, he began to tell me of the experiences he and friends had suffered at the cottage.

'It was built about a hundred and fifty years ago as a crofters' cottage', he said, but later occupants had added some rooms to the tiny building. 'That was about fifteen years ago.'

The actor had been told by some friends that their experiences in the cottage had convinced them that the building was haunted, but he believed these tales were caused by auto suggestion or sheer imagination until experiencing an incident in 1973 which really scared him.

The phenomena which had created the stories was the smell of newly-baked bread and toast very early in the morning which wafted round the site of the old long-sealed baking oven. This was noticed so frequently that a group of friends staying in the cottage decided to hold a seance with the aid of an upturned wine glass. 'A damned silly procedure' was the comment, with which I heartily agreed.

The only information gained from the party game was that a 'Miss Hathfield' used to live there and in common with many, if not all, villagers of the time she made her own bread. But the owner was reluctant to accept the name as genuine for it resembled so closely the name of the nearby village of Heathfield and felt that the coincidence was too great to bear credence.

Personally though, I could see no reason for this attitude, knowing of a Sir William Taunton of Taunton.

However the phenomena was to gain in strength and frequency until Miss Hathfield's phantom baking exploits were finally experienced by the owner himself. Early one morning the actor not only smelt the tantalising odour of baking bread, but heard faint and indistinguishable noises near the oven.

'I could no longer dismiss the stories' he told me, 'but another peculiar incident occurred in 1972.'

Three of his colleagues were staying the weekend and, whilst watching their host on a popular television programme in one of the most recently added rooms, heard the sound of a bell. One of the older gentlemen called to his son, 'there's the telephone', but on picking up the instrument the bell sounded again. Beside the television set, among other ornamental souvenirs, was a red glass bell and when the younger guest picked it up and rang it the others confirmed the sound that they had heard had been duplicated. Yet the bell had not moved and all three men were practically looking at it, being only inches away from the television screen.

This inexplicable mystery was never repeated, perhaps to the relief of everyone concerned.

One of the most awesome incidents which still remains in

vivid detail in the mind of the actor occurred one afternoon.

He was standing in a bedroom contemplating what action to take over a particular wall cupboard. 'I didn't know whether to repaint it, strip it down to the old wood or just throw it away'. Suddenly he sensed rather than heard someone coming up the stairs behind him and enter the room. There was nobody in the house at the time and as he turned round to see who the visitor was the bedroom door slowly closed.

'I'm afraid I just ran down the stairs into the garden out of sheer panic.'

Partially confirming the existence of someone unseen who frequents the bedroom is the fact that the actor's dog flatly refuses to go anywhere near the room.

Outside in the garden again I was shown a large wooden water butt containing barely an inch of water. 'Let's try to move it'. With our combined efforts the tub shifted a couple of inches away from the wall. Early one morning in 1972 when it was full of water the butt was found empty and lying on its side. This incident was repeated in June 1973. The barrel, situated some nine inches from the junction of two walls, is on York paving stone and leans slightly towards the house, away from the direction in which it was found.

Shortly after these incidents, the owner was puzzled by finding a complete loaf of bread floating on top of the now water-filled barrel. Was it, one wonders, Miss Hathfield's physical comment of rebuke about the modern baking methods? Some of the old country folk were and still are known for their outspoken feelings and it would not be surprising for a lonely old soul to express her utter disgust at the atomic-age bread by throwing one of the samples into a water butt.

As the actor and I stood together in the summer sunshine looking at that quiet secluded cottage, hidden away as it is from the sounds and sight of modern horrors and the pollution of car fumes, it was easy to recall the earlier days of quietness, politeness and individuality. A tiny stream trickled its way down one side of the garden, winding through moss-covered banks, ancient ferns and brambled hedgerows.

Behind the cottage a small group of cows contentedly munched their way through lush grass and buttercups, presenting a scene of unadulterated charm.

Does Miss Hathfield still walk the narrow path leading to the field beyond? Does she stand looking over the old lichen covered gate admiring the beauty of the untouched landscape, those soft gentle slopes of the green fields of Sussex? If so, we don't blame her. We could not even blame her for returning to her old bedroom or for throwing away a new loaf of chalk and bleached flour, but pushing over a huge water-filled barrel is not the sort of action suitable for a little old country lady. Unsuitable, but perhaps understandable.

There is the fact that the water butt is situated immediately in front of the original back door, now sealed up. But if that rear entrance was still accessible a person opening the door from the inside of the house could perhaps with a great deal of pushing aided by the leverage of the door itself create enough force to tip over the barrel.

Sited as it is, the storage unit would make it impossible for anyone to use the original entrance to the kitchen. If Miss Hathfield continues to make her spectral bread she would be more than annoyed at finding her immediate access to the garden blocked by a huge water barrel. Could it be therefore that phantom forces have been harnessed to aid the wraith of that independent old character?

We continued to discuss the olden days compared with the so-called benefits of today's money race until the time came for me to depart.

Looking back once more at the ancient old thatch and the delightful peaceful countryside, I really wondered if Miss Hathfield was better off than the current owner, troubled and harrassed as we all are by the continuing rising costs of just living.

CHAPTER 9

ROBERTSBRIDGE AND MOUNTFIELD

Visitors may wonder what it is that attracts so many person-
alities to such a small rural village community as Robertsbridge. Here amidst the rapidly vanishing hops, the gentle
curves of the surrounding hills, and the sheep and cattle
covered fields reside national figures such as Malcolm Mugge-
ridge, Harry Andrews, the film and television actor, Illing-
worth, the renowned cartoonist, Eira Heath, a popular television singing star and, more recently Tom Jones and
Englebert Humperdinck who have purchased one of the
larger farms of the village.

The arts, too, are well represented with sculptors, painters,
writers and even one of the few designers of silverware.

Is it the charm of the environment, the friendliness of the
villagers or the ideal location which brings in so many
strangers to the country life? Most probably it is a combination of all three.

The medieval village lies tucked into the valleys carved by
the junction of the rivers Rother and Darwell and the
Glottenham stream. Two of these waterways provided the
motive power for Bugsell and Robertsbridge Mills, now long
since inoperative.

The village itself relies on its formation from the foundation
of the Cistercian Abbey created by Robert de St Martin in
1176 at a time when the river Rother was navigable right
down to the coast at Rye. A huge rusting anchor displayed

in *The Seven Stars,* one of the oldest buildings in the village, acts as a reminder of the early days.

Part of the ruins of the original abbey are incorporated into a private house now on the outskirts of the village, for development of the community took place nearly two miles to the west. This site, the cross roads with the main road from Tunbridge Wells to Hastings and the route to Brightling, formed the ideal spot for the natural growth of the small group of peasants drawn into the neighbourhood by the activity of the friars.

North east of the village centre, at the bottom of a lane leading to Bodiam, lies Bourne Farm which Leonard Hodson in his *Short History of Salehurst* claims 'for many years enjoyed the reputation of being haunted', but was unable to provide any details of the phenomena.

Only a mile to the north the traveller finds the former community of Northbridge Street and to the east the church of St Mary at Salehurst which serves the area. Here in the 1930s a nurse was killed when cycling to attend to one of her patients.

Unheeding of the stormy night she speeded her cycle down the hill but at the bend outside the gateway she skidded, swerved and fell breaking her neck. Once or twice since then the occasional stroller walking up the hill has been surprised to see the silent figure of a woman, apparently in a cloak, rushing towards them only to vanish at the church gates.

Because of the lie of the land and the abundance of water which practically surrounds the village, the lower areas of Robertsbridge have frequently been flooded with the occasional resultant death by drowning, but none quite so tragic as that of a young girl who fell into the Glottenham stream. The most recent occasion when some of the cottages and even modern buildings suffered from flood waters was in 1973 bringing the usual concern to the village as the Rother once again spread itself over fields which so many hundreds of years ago formed the river bed. The incident also brought back recollections of the young girl whose body was found washed up against one of the cottages behind the shops in the High Street some forty years earlier.

As on past occasions, within days of the floods receding, at least one resident saw the pathetic wraith of the small white figure of the child gliding up from the stream to the back door of her former home.

A few yards from the road leading to Salehurst, on the east side, a terrace of three little cottages face the main road. Reports of a phantom man having been seen in earlier days in one of these cottages hints of some unfortunate accident, perhaps connected with the flooding.

Continue walking south towards Battle and one passes on the left the Wealden house now converted into a popular pub called *The Seven Stars*. It is here that phantom footsteps are heard walking across an empty room above the public bar.

The building itself was constructed in 1380, just thirty years after the earliest music manuscript associated with the abbey was written, but it has other associations with the religious house. There are always rumours of tunnels leading to or from churches, castles and the like, but seldom are such claims substantiated. The tunnel leading from *The Seven Stars* to the abbey however has been confirmed, for within living memory one of the regular visitors to the pub walked some two hundred feet inside the ancient construction. He only stopped and returned 'because the air was getting a bit thin'.

The mysterious footsteps are popularly linked with 'the ghost of the Red Monk of Robertsbridge', and it was only in 1972 that it is believed he was seen in recent times by a stranger. A Canadian girl on holiday staying at the pub asked Ruth Parkes, wife of the licensee, who the monk was that she had seen when going to the bathroom during the night. But there were no other people staying that night in the pub, yet the girl was convinced she had seen a figure gliding along the corridor dressed in a long dark cloak.

The pub also houses a mysterious shaft some seventy feet deep leading from the loft straight down to the cellars and the tunnel entrance. Was this peculiar vent connected perhaps with the smuggling 'profession' which was rife in the area? Remembering that the abbey was at one time on the banks of the river it would not be surprising for smuggling gangs to off-load some of their booty near the abbey, perhaps goods ostensibly for the villagers, and then to transport it through the tunnel to the safety of the loft in the pub.

The Seven Stars also boasts of a minute room in which, it is claimed, Charles II was kept hidden when a boy and adjoining it is a small, practically vertical, flight of stairs to the attic and the top entrance of the shaft beside the chimney breast. Legend also has it that the legalities regarding the ransom of Richard I were conducted here and the King presented a font to Salehurst Church as a thank-offering for the work carried out by the Abbot of Robertsbridge. The font, probably the same age as the church, is adorned with a salamander motif similar to that on the font in Winchester Cathedral.

On the opposite side of the road in *The Grange,* a large house, now an antique shop, sounds of ghostly childrens' voices have been heard near the main staircase.

The visitor is now within a few yards of *The George* and the former site of the village green, most of which is now taken up by the war memorial—one of the ugliest edifices in the village—and the car park of the pub. On the right, however, a cluster of timbered cottages offers one of the most attractive sights to the casual visitor. The end building was in former years another of the village's pubs but it has now reverted to the charm of a private home.

The George, a seventeenth-century inn renowned for its food and friendliness, also has a phantom, heard as inexplicable bumps in the large room over the bars. The room is used for wedding receptions and general meetings of local organisations and the belief is that the ghost is somehow aggrieved with marriage for the weird noises are only heard after a reception has been held there. The room itself is a large one, but from its appearance was once two bedrooms. The noises 'like someone with his legs tied together trying to move around the empty room' are usually heard at lunchtime, but the phantom's existence has also been associated with the mysterious movement of objects elsewhere in the building.

Opposite *The George* is another of the village's really attractive properties and one which doubles as a branch library, the Youth Employment Bureau, the meeting place of the old people's club and the youth club.

Shortly after a new deputy youth leader had been appointed, he was travelling in from Battle and noticed a light in an upstairs window. 'The building should have been empty at that time of day and I was puzzled for a moment. Then I assumed someone had inadvertently left the light on, but as I drove past I saw the face of an old woman peering out. I drove round the corner to park my car and came back only to find the light out and the place locked up. When I opened up I went all over the building but it was empty so I forgot the incident'.

Later that evening the deputy enquired from the other staff as to whom the little old lady could have been and was more than a little surprised to learn that he had described the former owner of the house before the county council had bought it. She had died many years ago. No other incidents have been reported, but one feels that a man, more or less a stranger to the area, could hardly imagine the phantom of someone he had never met or knew had existed.

Continue up the hill, passing the council estate of Heathfield Gardens, past Browns Farmhouse and one reaches Busheygate, home of the author. The building was originally a pair of tied farm cottages constructed in 1725 on the Egerton Estate and existed as such until 1970 when, having lain empty for a couple of years, they were sold to an elderly gentleman from Heathfield. He hoped to persuade his elderly girl friend to join him and proposed to add a new wing at the back to accommodate the bathroom and kitchen. However, the lady refused and the property was once again put on to the market, and I purchased it two months later. The house lies immediately opposite Poppinghole Lane, mentioned in documents of the time of the Domesday Book as 'Poppa haeoth', Poppa's heath, which formed part of the fifth-century manor of Popmoor, long since vanished.

There is some evidence that Busheygate may have been constructed on the site of a medieval building, though historians claim that there was no mention of it on maps of the time. Adze marks appear on many of the exposed timbers and a pair of medieval slippers were found in 1971 when the floor level of one of the cottages had to be lowered. The building is also in a direct line from the abbey to the site of the medieval castellated villa of Glottenham, nearly two miles away.

Adding strength to the idea of an earlier building on the site is that the house faces due south and a traveller coming from Poppinghole desiring to visit the villa would walk along what was a public footpath in front of the building and then down through the fields to Glottenham. The footpath was closed in 1934.

One day, shortly after purchasing the cottages and during the period when builders were at work converting the property, I was working in the garden reconstructing the path round the front of the house. Suddenly I heard footsteps of someone approaching, but because I was balancing a very large slab of York stone at that moment said 'hang on a minute. I'll just get this laid and I'll be with you'. The stone was laid but on looking up to greet my visitor, I found the garden empty. There have been numerous occasions when visitors to the house have 'felt' and 'half seen' a figure watching them from the corner of the garage and a couple of people gazing at the house from the south hedge.

On a visit to the local pub shortly after my arrival I was asked if I had seen the ghost of 'the lady in white' in the garden, but the questioner had no knowledge of who she might be.

It was perhaps unfortunate that to form the new home it was necessary to destroy two old baking ovens, for a mystery was revealed when opening one of the ovens. Sealed into the roof, against the dividing wall, lay an ancient rust-covered carving knife, only a couple of feet from where the slippers had been found.

One of the first visitors to the cottage after conversion was a clairvoyant who claimed that 'something unpleasant was associated with the site of the oven' and later, handling the knife, described the murder of a young woman in the woods near the castle site, 'but her body was brought back here'. In the newly-formed corridor immediately above the oven site another visitor was apprehensive about a feeling of 'diabolical horror' which was concentrated there. The spot would once have been the corner of a double bedroom and one can only assume that the feeling is so strong that the two areas are affected.

Several complete strangers have visited the building and many of them are struck by the atmosphere at the same spot: in May 1975 two visitors of a party of six were so overcome that they fainted, and a water diviner informed me that there was a skeleton buried in exactly the same place.

Another mystery experienced by myself and numerous guests is the smell of strong tobacco at about 5.30pm near one of the inglenook fireplaces. A reporter from LBC Radio appeared quite frightened at experiencing the sudden smell of pipe tobacco when conducting an interview in 1974.

One day, in some ancient dusty document, the answer to the mystery may be revealed, but meanwhile let us continue on the road to the coast.

Two miles further south on the Battle Road beyond John's Cross lies Mountfield, shown as 'Mundfield' on ancient maps.

To the right lies the well-known gypsum mines, producing a major portion of Britain's plaster and alabaster as well as roadstone and basic compounds for a variety of purposes.

On the left a narrow opening leads to Riverhall Farm and a few yards further on lies a tiny workers' cottage overlooking the main farmhouse. It was built late in the 1700s to house a pair of families. In those days privacy was not as important as today for joining the two homes is the shared staircase with only one room either side. A modern improvement has been the addition of a kitchen at the back of the building looking out through a lean-to conservatory.

Not only was the staircase shared between the tenant workers but also, it seems, the garden with the farmer, for nowhere are there clear-cut boundaries but merely a footpath from the farmhouse drive up to the back door of the cottage.

Many years ago, however, a lane led north from the front garden through South Park Wood to Vinehall and the Hastings road and south to a spinney, now owned by the Forestry Commission. Although the path can still be seen it is now so overgrown as to be impassable.

Some time during 1937 William Clarke, a retired school-master from Bristol, bought the house and with a partner, Mr Verrall a solicitor, intended to learn how to run and manage a small dairy farm.

Clarke, described by a former tenant of a bungalow on the estate as 'short and sharp and thin-looking and with a character to match', lived with his wife and daughter in the farmhouse, planning and learning. Most of the information on how to run the farm however seemed to be provided by Bill Woods, a tenant of Riverhall Farm Cottage.

Bill had never been closely connected with farming but he was knowledgeable and had created a striking impression on William. Everything Woods suggested was carried out, every piece of advice was acted upon—he was considered the expert.

But the farm went through bad times: animals died and

the crops failed. But Woods was not to be blamed, for there was a strong element of bad luck, be it bad weather or other misfortune.

Clarke grew more morose, more worried, more short-tempered with everyone except, of course, his adviser. He would spend hours with Woods in his tiny cottage discussing and debating what action to take over the latest disaster. Every time some new problem arose, the farmer, with some surly comment to his family, would storm out and stride purposefully up the little path to find solace and an answer.

The situation began to appear irretrievable. Mrs and Miss Clarke, realising the appalling situation, begged William to sell up before bankruptcy caused complete collapse of the farm and utter ruin to the family.

For several days Clarke was silent. Then one Tuesday afternoon in March 1953 after an 'unholy row' with his wife and daughter he took his little black Austin 6 car to the local service station at John's Cross. 'Fill her up' was his curt demand. The forecourt attendant was used to Clarke's moods and silently complied, filling the tank with petrol. 'Give me a quart of oil', the customer growled. The can was produced and the payment made.

The farmer then drove back to Riverhall where he 'messed about in his garage for some time'. It was during this period he closed up the points on two plugs of the car engine and poured the oil into the petrol tank, though for what purpose was a mystery at the time.

By nine o'clock that night he was once again with Bill Woods but what was said will never be known. Did he at last realise that the chaos he and his family suffered had been caused by his own failure to take responsibility in a business that has such frequent ups and downs at the best of times? Did he finally blame Woods for the disaster or did he try desperately to reach some satisfactory answer to the problems which engulfed him and his life?

At 9.40 he lifted the latch of Bill's sitting-room door for

the last time. 'I must go'. The door swung open and he stumbled through, giving a vicious swipe with his twisted and gnarled walking stick at the panelling. A few minutes later he was back with his family who by now had realised something was wrong.

William slumped into a chair throwing his stick to the floor with a movement which showed his utter despair. He sat there silent for some time. Suddenly, as if making up his mind about some appalling decision, he picked up his stick, growled, 'just going to check up round the buildings', and walked out. The time was 10.20. He was never seen alive again.

By the early hours his family, desperate with anxiety as to his whereabouts, had called the police, friends and neighbours in an attempt to find him. At about seven o'clock on Wednesday morning a signalman walking along the rail track to the Battle Road level crossing saw a black Austin car in the woods at the side of the track and reported the strange position of the vehicle to a policeman in a passing patrol car.

The asphyxiated body of sixty-seven-year old William Clarke lay slumped over the wheel. He was identified later by his partner.

The Clarkes continued on at Riverhall for only six months before finding a new buyer for the farm and moving away, away from the site of their personal disaster. Shortly after the new owner took over the shambles of the small farming community Bill Woods moved out.

In April 1971 Anne Burnaby and her friend Tint Errington-Kitching moved into Bill's former home and within a few weeks of occupation had been puzzled when sitting in their lounge by seeing the latch of the door lift up and the door itself swing open. 'There was no regularity about it, but when we started to note the incidents we found that it always happened at 9.40pm. Never at any other time'.

One evening a friend staying for the week-end and watching television by herself suddenly heard a noise near the front door and loking up saw the figure of 'a little old man with a wizened face leaning on a peculiar twisted walking stick standing in the corner'. She later described him as being 'quite short, but thin and with rather an aggressive expression'. Having looked at the wraith for a second 'he just faded away, leaving rather a cold feeling in the room'. Who was it, she wanted to know.

Miss Burnaby mentioned the experience and the incidents concerning the door to a neighbour who thought that they must be caused by Mr Jarvis who hung himself in the spinney about two hundred years ago. The current owners of the cottage temporarily accepted this as the probable cause, but the door continued to be opened 'fairly frequently, about once a fortnight'. However, on making further enquiries, the couple were assured that the invisible phantom of Mr Jarvis had nothing to do with the phenomena. The clues which established the identity of the spectre were the full description of the phantom with his walking stick and the time of the incidents. It could only have been the ghost of Mr Clarke. As soon as this was realised the incidents stopped, never to be repeated. 'William has been recognised and can now rest in peace' is the belief expressed and one that I think is probably correct.

But an unanswerable question could be raised. Did the death of Mr Jarvis, one of the original tenants in the eighteenth century who committed suicide in the woods, have any effect on the fatal decision made some two hundred years later by Mr Clarke?

CHAPTER 10

RYE AND WINCHELSEA

It must be difficult in the twentieth century for a town as ancient as Rye to retain its character and individuality, yet not only does it continue to offer a variety of historical and interesting facets to thousands of tourists, but also continues its possession of distinct qualities and attractive charm.

I always welcome the opportunity to visit Rye with its Ypres Tower sold in 1430 to raise money, the beautiful Church of St Mary, famous for its eighteenth-century quarter boys, but above all the cobbled Mermaid Street. This lane, typical of a medieval town contains the notable Old Hospital, a fifteenth-century building, and several Georgian houses built on thirteenth-century foundations.

Rye was, like Winchelsea, linked through history to the confederation of the five Cinque Ports as an Ancient Town and thus boasts the unique privilege of granting freeman the title of 'baron'.

The origin of the Cinque Ports is wreathed in mystery for they were in existence long before the Norman Conquest and, it seems, were a guild of seaman who fished not only from the head ports of Sussex and Kent but also controlled the herring industry of Yarmouth. Such was the control there that despite becoming a free borough in 1209 Yarmouth had to suffer the Cinque Port barons holding court during the annual fair until ceasing their rights in 1663.

The town of Rye was granted to the Abbey of Fecamp in Normandy by King Canute, a factor which may have influenced William in choosing Pevensey as his invasion bridgehead. Following the loss of Normandy in 1204 it became dangerous to allow the major ports of Rye and Winchelsea

to be controlled by the Norman abbot and so in 1247 Chelten-
ham and parts of Lincolnshire were offered in exchange.

The Ypres Tower, relic of the thirteenth century, is so-
called because of its granting to the de Ipres family in the
fifteenth century but some three hundred years later it had
become the borough gaol and used to house French prisoners.
I found supporting evidence of this when, during one of my
many visits there, for it is now a fascinating little museum, I
discovered an old French coin in one of the rose beds which
now decorate the former exercise yard.

Walk back down over the cobbles towards the centre of the
town through Pump Street into East Street and Conduit Hill
to the Augustine Friary, known now as 'Cinque Ports Pottery'.
This monks' house was orginally situated in 1265 on the
eastern side of the town in Ockman's Lane at the end of the
High Street, but in common with a lot of buildings and part
of the old town wall it was destroyed by the action of the
sea cutting away the cliff. The current building is the chancel
of the friary church constructed in 1379.

In 1762 excavations were carried out on a plot at the side
to lay down foundations for a new wall and during the work
parts of several skeletons were discovered and assumed to be
connected with the friary. In 1940, nearly two hundred years
later, further digging was required to provide air-raid shelters
and it was with considerable surprise and shock that the
workmen, nearing the old foundation floor of the monastery,
realised that they had opened an unusual mass grave.
Skeletons of fourteen men were revealed but all were found
upright in a kneeling position. So far no one has offered any
rational explanation for the mystery. Who were the men?
What killed them? Were they unbelievably buried alive and
if so, why?

As I peered at the car park which covers that horrible site
of death I recalled the oft quoted tale of Brother 'Cantator',
so named because of his 'divine singing'. Despite his vows and
strict religious training this young monk was unfortunate

enough to fall in love with a beautiful young girl named Amanda. This youngster lived in the Dormy House, now a club and an interesting old building sited conveniently behind the friary facing out over the desolate marshland stretching to the modern harbour of Rye.

Brother Cantator attempted to control his emotions and overwhelming passion for the attractive wench, but when she indicated that his love was returned his defences collapsed and they decided to escape the bonds and wrath of the church by eloping across the Channel. Hurriedly, but stealthily, they made their plans and prepared for the departure.

But somehow their scheme was discovered. No doubt an indiscreet word or careless action had betrayed them. So-called justice was swift. The abbot had the foolish monk brought before him and declared that his actions and intentions had destroyed the reputation of the brotherhood and broken the strict but accepted laws of the friary. Death was to be the punishment. 'Cantator' would be bricked up in his cell alive so that he could contemplate on his crime and pray that his soul would eventually be cleansed.

The brother pleaded and begged for his life, for release from the vows he had taken. It was to no avail. He was dragged to his minute room and thrown against the wall for there would be no room for him to lie down. Propped against the stones, half conscious, the young man could have had no strength left to fight. The walling-in was completed.

For days the brothers of the friary heard the cries and the moans, the shrieks and the pleadings of their dying brother. They heard him talking, then singing and finally a weird gobbling noise as his mind cracked under the mental and physical torture. The bubbling, choking sounds seemed to last for days, but eventually grew quieter and softer. Then finally peace and silence. Brother Cantator was dead.

In the nineteenth century a few residents strolling in the evening along Hilders Cliff or up Conduit Hill were puzzled at hearing the sounds of a turkey gobbling. The mystery was short-lived for someone suddenly recalled the manner in which a monk had died because of his love for a local girl. But by then a narrow alleyway from which the sounds seemed to emanate had been termed as Turkey Cock Lane, forever reminding the populace of the fate which befell a monk some five hundred years ago. It is possible that the actual site of the death cell is below the foundations of the congregational church built in 1894.

The incident can never be forgotten either by Rye or a Miss Marjorie Pillars of Surrey who, when staying with friends in a guest house during the Easter holiday of 1952, was quietly sitting in the corner of a sitting-room drinking an afternoon cup of tea. She heard a faint sound and looking up saw the figure of a monk in a brown habit standing by the party wall of the next-door property.

She was puzzled, but politely ignored initially the sudden arrival at what she thought was a new guest or visitor. Then, surreptitiously studying the man more closely, she realised that he looked very ill and was swaying slightly. Not wishing to embarrass him, she resumed her tea break, but minutes later she glanced at the corner again, only to find that the figure had gone. Only then did she realise that what she had observed was a phantom and it was many years before she learnt of the history of the locality.

The party wall of the house next door, the Dormy House, was known to have been moved a few feet from the neighbouring property in the eighteenth century and it was this action which probably resulted in the figure of what can be presumed to be Brother 'Cantator' being seen. 'How pitiful he looked', said Miss Pillars. 'I felt so sorry for him.'

One wonders what specific incident caused him to return once more to the home of his mistress, but I should imagine that it was the recollection of the fatal day when he arrived to break the appalling news of discovery to Amanda. The shock he must have suffered and the fear of the results will continue to haunt the area for some time to come.

I walked back into the High Street towards The Mint and up Lion Street towards the church. Before continuing to the famous *Mermaid Inn* I called in at the *Fletchers House* restaurant for a cup of tea. It was here that John Fletcher, contemporary of William Shakespeare, was born in 1579. The house was a private home for many hundreds of years, having accommodated the Fletchers for only a short period, but became an eating house in 1932.

Few alterations have been carried out and even its original front door with carvings of Tudor and York roses over the lintel have been retained. This door is a reminder of the days when it was the local vicarage facing the church. John Fletcher's father, the Reverend Richard Fletcher, having lived there for many years on the understanding that he would eventually be appointed vicar of Rye finally lost patience and moved away when his son was only two years old. The existing vicar, the Reverend Connope, despite a long absence had flatly refused to resign his position and the church in desperation sold the property on the open market.

The restaurant itself is usually crowded with tourists, but out of season the friendly pleasant atmosphere and good food attracts many local actors, writers and artists. One of the most interesting rooms is the large dining-room upstairs with the huge fireplace and a very ancient cupboard or wardrobe.

Another smaller staircase leads to a room at the top of the house used by the management as an office and it was here at 4 o'clock one afternoon in 1951 that Mrs Betty Howard, the sister of the owner, was working on the accounts. After about half an hour of dealing with the problems of balancing the books she suddenly heard footsteps on the stairs and, thinking that a customer had lost his way, opened the door to find out who it was.

Standing on the landing a few feet below her was a young man in a dark Edwardian lounge suit. He was in his thirties she told me 'and was quite six feet tall'. Mrs Howard greeted the stranger and asked if she could help him. At that moment the apparition just faded away, and disappeared completely. I was assured by the owner that, although the phantom was never seen again, sounds resembling footsteps walking up the stairway are occasionally heard by members of the staff when the shop is closed. Who the visitor was or why he frequents the house can probably never be established, but he frightens nobody and is accepted as just another ghost of Rye.

Finishing my refreshment I continued my journey to the world famous Mermaid Street and its equally renowned inn. One writer, Arthur Gaunt, in *Tourist England* claims that Mermaid Street 'is the old-fashioned street in an old-fashioned town' of a formerly well-known song. Unfortunately for the reader he continues a hundred pages later to state that Watchbell Street is the original site, but whichever is correct the area achieved notoriety in the eighteenth century when Rye and the surrounding countryside was the centre of smuggling in the south east. The headquarters of the audacious Collins gang was the *Market Cross* at Alfriston and the *Starre and Crown* at Goudhurst housed the murderous Hawkhurst gang, except when they were near Rye when they would use *The Mermaid*.

These bands of armed smugglers would frequently ride through the streets like cowboys of the West discharging their pistols in all directions with utter abandon. Why such thieving, murdering rogues ever gained the popularity that they achieved is hard to understand. Perhaps it was their complete disregard for the law and authority which endeared them to the locals, or it might have been the courage which they showed and the crafty devices they used to prevent capture which warranted admiration.

The date of the construction of the inn is obscure though claims are made that French raiders burnt down the original *Mearmeade* in 1377. The town was sacked and burnt in 1339 and 1360 as well and scorch marks from these attacks can still be seen on stones of St Mary's Church. There is certainly evidence that the current building was in existence as early as

1636, but it is also known that it was originally constructed as a private house in the fifteenth century and probably dates from 1420. But adding strength to the belief of even earlier days the cellars have been dated as thirteenth century.

By 1758 it had reverted to private use and remained so for over a century when it became a club. In 1945 *The Mermaid* reopened as a public house and popular hotel.

Through its chequered history *The Mermaid* has been altered and modified numerous times and practically every time fresh evidence of smugglers and highwaymen's activities has been revealed. A secret staircase, a hidden wall, a priest's hole and an underground tunnel all have their place in the medieval hostelry.

There are two stories of ghosts here. One of a local girl who was in love with one of the smugglers, but because of her insistence at being with her man at all times the girl proved an embarrassing liability and was murdered. She still wanders the corridors of the inn, unable to accept her punishment. The other tale is of an experience by Mrs Aldington who awoke one October night to find two phantoms fighting a silent duel in the bedroom. The swordsmen, dressed in doublets and hose, fought for some seconds until one obviously received a fatal blow. The victor glanced apprehensively round the room and pulled the bleeding form of his adversary to a trap door in a corner of the floor. He opened the aperture and dropped the body through into what was a secret underground dungeon.

Completing my admiration of the other ancient houses in the cobbled street including the old hospital, I returned to the car park on the site of the town ditch and abutting part of the old wall erected in 1194 and began the short drive to Rye's twin town, Winchelsea.

Here, parking the car in a road adjoining the ruins of St Thomas's Church, I recalled my previous visit in 1970 when I had been mystified by the clattering sound of horses' hooves on the road.

The old town was overwhelmed by the sea at the end of the thirteenth century, but preparations for its reconstruction on its present hilltop position had already been completed to a plan of Edward I. Three of the original gates remain but little evidence of the walls which encircled the town.

In the fourteenth century Winchelsea was more prosperous than Rye, though walking through its streets today it is difficult to accept this. Compared with the now larger town, it is more of a village with so few shops that a visitor would wonder from where the residents obtain their supplies, yet at its zenith it was a major fishing port concentrating on the importing of wine from France.

It is for this reason that there are some thirty medieval vaulted cellars still to be found below the older houses. The finest example is beneath a home formerly *The Salutation Inn,* one of the many pubs which opened to deal with the population of some six thousand people.

By the beginning of the sixteenth century Winchelsea's value as a port was gone and the last merchant left. Practically derelict and deserted, the town diminished both in size and power, becoming a mere stopping place for travellers to Rye and Hastings, but a rather unsavoury and dangerous one.

Two remaining revered gentlemen of the town in the eighteenth century were the Weston brothers who lived there gaining an excellent reputation for their honour and exemplary conduct. What was not realised about the brothers was that these two characters changed overnight into a pair of 'Mr Hydes'.

Stealing horses, stopping and robbing coaches travelling to the bigger towns and carrying out an intense smuggling campaign were but some of the crimes of this evil pair. It was not until 1782 that the Westons were caught and executed.

But at least one of them remains in the locality and, it seems, is accompanied by some of his stolen goods.

Under a tree, near the walls of the Church of St Thomas,

George Weston used to wait for his brother, the expert in horse stealing. He often had to kick his heels for a couple of hours, depending on the route that John took and the interest taken by the law in a group of horses being led by one man up the hill from the Rye road into Winchelsea.

Luck and life had been good to them both. They were prosperous and respected wine merchants trading in Rye, Hastings and in their own town. Their night-time activities provided the thrill of breaking the law and the extra cash needed to keep their families 'well breeched'. Few had any suspicions about their huge stocks of high quality brandy and other spirits, so large at one time that they had to ask friends to lend them their wine cellars.

It is probable that the genuine duty paid liquor was stored only in the Westons' vaults whilst the illicit bottles gathered dust and value in the unsuspecting neighbours' properties.

George Weston, the real highwayman, used the sanctity of the churchyard tree to await the arrival of the Hastings coach. As soon as he heard it approaching he would don his mask and gallop forth to stop and challenge the scared occupants, threatening with immediate death unless they delivered all their wealth.

It was in 1970, that, following a visit to the small but interesting Winchelsea museum, I was preparing to return to my hotel in Rye. I was just on the point of turning right towards the Strand Gate when I heard the sounds of a number of horses galloping up the hill and through the gateway. I reversed the car and waited for the animals to pass me expecting to see them come into view at any moment.

The sound stopped as suddenly as it started. Puzzled, I walked to the corner. There was nothing in sight, just an empty street. It was only later did I learn that my experience was that of a number of people who had heard the noises of what is believed to be a group of horses stolen by the Weston brothers.

I glanced again towards the church and the trees bending

gently in the afternoon breeze. What was that beneath one of them? Was it shadow, or was it a man on horseback? If it were a man he was headless as was George Weston when he died. I stared harder. No—it was merely a shadow. I had not been one of those lucky enough to see the phantom smuggler. He has been seen only infrequently and I cannot be lucky all the time.

I returned to the car and drove home slightly envious of the tranquility enjoyed by those peaceful folk of Winchelsea, and wondering if all the bottles of wine hidden by those two crooks some three hundred years ago have been discovered.

CHAPTER 11

PASHLEY MANOR, TICEHURST

'Is it real?' asked my companion as we approached Pashley Manor peeping between the branches of a magnificent oak tree. The black timbers in stark contrast to the white plaster and the design of the ancient house resembled some film director's dream for a Jacobean film set, the ideal site for a gruesome murder or the haunting by a grey lady. Both in fact apply.

Pashley offers a glorious view of Brightling Beacon 'Fuller's Folly' and gentle valleys cuddling the little river Lymden in the foreground. In earlier days it was approached by an avenue direct from the main road to Ticehurst and Hurst Green but now there is a winding drive through the park offering intriguing glimpses of the ancient home.

Unlike some old houses it consists only of a combination of three periods. About a third of the house, behind the older front, is a huge Georgian addition of 1730 whilst its face, now stripped of Victorian appendages and so-called improvements, reveals a sixteenth-century countenance. Meanwhile the cellars display a probable thirteenth-century foundation.

The outlines and proportions of the east side bears a very strong resemblance to another historical building, that of Brickwell at Northiam but its links with royalty are much stronger.

The manor takes its name from the Passelewe family, Robert being one of the first owners. He was Archdeacon of

Lewes and in 1232 became Treasurer of the Exchequer. His brother Simon also held many judicial posts including that of Justice of the Jews and in 1268 he was named as Baron of the Exchequer employed on exhorting financial support from religious houses for the benefit of Henry III.

It was due to Robert's influence that Sir Edmund de Passele acquired a vast amount of property in Kent and Sussex and evidence of this can be seen in the original Charter of Free Warren granted to Sir Edmund in 1317 and now held by Mrs Margaret Cole, a descendant of the family who owned Pashley in the sixteenth century.

Although this document is the first connection between the Pashleys and Ticehurst, Elias and Giles de Passeley are mentioned on a deed relating to property in Robertsbridge, dated 1185. There is a strong belief that the first house was that of a hunting lodge built on an island in the largest of the three ponds below the southern face of the manor. The pond itself has for centuries been termed as 'the moat', but any sign of an earlier building is hidden by the cluster of trees and shrubs on the island.

It was in 1327 on Sir Edmund's death that certain events occurred which were to affect Pashley and its occupants for some years.

Robert, eldest son of Sir Edmund, had been granted the property but only ten days before the sudden and mysterious death of his father and brother William the heir on 1 March 1327. Edmund had appointed his wife Margaret as chief executor of his will and the Prior of Holy Trinity at Hastings as her assistant.

But criminal proceedings were taken out which affected Margaret and legal disputes, long contested, were to delay the final settlement of the estate. One of the reasons for this situation was that Edmund had two wives.

Margaret was either a widow or, as suggested by Lindsay Fleming, the wife of William de Basing, and appears to have taken the place of 'second string' for his first companion had been a Maud de Kechenore. On Maud's death, however, Edmund married Joan, so he was either a bigamist or Margaret was not his legal wife.

Quite rightly under the cirmcumstances Joan petitioned the King, Edward III, stating that Margaret, wife of William Basing, was living with Edmund 'impurely'. The knight was charged to return to Joan but Margaret, realising that the obvious outcome would be the loss of the estate, poisoned both her 'husband' and William, his eldest son by Maud. The villainous woman 'did then murder Edmund, Joan's son, aged thirteen and John Walet his groom at Colesdon in Surrey'.

The legal wife took no action for some years but sued for dower. Several court cases resulted from the murder and a writ was issued for Margaret's arrest, but when the sheriff's party arrived at Pashley Manor a crowd assaulted the officials who fled.

In April 1331 Margaret, having surrendered to the under-sheriff, escaping and surrendering again, was acquitted of procuring the murder.

So many disputes, so many legal battles and so many relatives were involved in the following twenty years that a book could be written about the Pashleys alone. It is sufficient to say that Margaret, the dominant character and heiress to the Normanvilles appears to have succeeded in her crimes. Evidence of her freedom is that she later became the companion of Simon le Mareshal.

In 1452 Sir John de Pashele of 'Great Pashele in Tysherst' died and two years later, during the War of the Roses, Sir Geoffrey and Thomas Bulleyn or Boleyn became the owners. However, they let it to a John Lewknor, but by 1489 Sir William Bulleyn was back in residence. His son Thomas held court at Pashley in 1518 and was later to become Earl of Wiltshire and Viscount Rochford.

By this time it is assumed the original 'house in the pond' had gone and the existing property established a few hundred yards away on higher ground. Thomas Bulleyn eventually married Elizabeth, daughter of Thomas Howard, the Earl of Surrey and fathered that famous daughter Ann. According to Strickland's *Queens* the future sovereign spent her earliest days at the family home at Blickling Hall in Norfolk, but reference is made to the fact that 'she came later to Hever Castle from Pashley', so at least one Queen of England has paced the grounds here.

Adding a further touch of royal interest to the ancient history of the manor is the fact that an Elizabeth Pashley married Reginald de Pympe. Elizabeth was closely related to Elizabeth of York, mother of Henry VIII whose elder daughter, Margaret of Scotland, is the lineal ancestress of the present royal family. The grandmother of the Pashley girl was Elizabeth Woodville whose mother, Jaquetta, Princess of Luxembourg, was 'so successful in intrigue that her power of the minds of men was popularly attributed to sorcery'. Her husband was 'the handsomest man in England'.

In 1539 Sir James Bulleyn, uncle of Ann, succeeded to the manor but for some reason only three years later he decided to sell Pashley to Thomas May of Combwell at a cost of £360. The estate then included 600 acres of land and a water mill with an iron furnace.

The May family who held Pashley for some three hundred years were reputed to be associated with the formation of the village of Mayfield and included Thomas, a writer and poet, who died through suffocation by tying his night cap too tightly. He was born at Mayfield in 1595, became a historian of the Long Parliament and was a great friend of Ben Jonson.

It was Anthony May who was responsible for the reconstruction of the Tudor house in 1621. He was a prominent figure in the county, being Sheriff of Sussex and owner of at least one iron mill, if not two. The direct descendants continued in occupation until 1796 when all the males having died the property passed to a daughter Caroline who married the Reverend Richard Wetherell.

Ownership remained with that branch until it came to a nephew, Doctor Gerald Wetherell Capon Hollist who died in 1922.

In about 1918 during the Hollist ownership there was considerable talk among the servants of 'the ghost' which had been seen by practically every member of the staff. One of the last to witness the phantom was Madge who told me that when she was in her teens as an under parlour maid she saw the 'lady in grey'. The maid was clearing up after a shooting party had returned to the house and was in a bedroom collecting the muddied boots for cleaning. She glanced up towards the open door and saw gliding along the front landing the figure of a woman with her arms swinging, as if walking with some considerable purpose on a special errand.

'She had white hair piled on her head rather like a bun', Madge told me. 'She wore a high-necked shirt blouse, shaped and gathered into a very small waist, but as she had just turned having come up the stairs I was unable to see her face'. There was an air of grace and charm about the apparition and certainly nothing to scare the young girl even though she was unable to see any legs. 'The figure just faded into nothingness at the waist', she said.

However she followed the ghost into the Violet Room, opposite the Oak Room where other members of the staff had been disturbed by the appearance, but on entering she found it completely empty. It was in the Oak Room that on one occasion, after a ball, a gown 'hung on a wardrobe to air' was knocked to the floor by an unseen entity.

In the same area, several members of the living-in staff had been frightened by being woken early in the morning by the ghost 'rattling the china' and knocking on two of the bedroom doors. It was with great relish that the cook described seeing 'on a winter's evening' a pair of 'phantom hands' grasping out through the balustrades at the top of the stairs.

Pashley was bought from the doctor's sister by Edwin King in 1922, but the house was to see few actual occupiers until

1945, though troops lived there for a brief period during the last war, causing some damage. Some of the apparent vandalism may have been caused by fear experienced by the young soldiers for there was at least one occasion when a group of them had been scared by seeing the 'phantom lady of the manor'.

By the end of hostilities Pashley Manor must have resembled a 'typical haunted house'. Ivy clinging to the old brickwork, dilapidated rotten wood work and an overgrown garden all merged to strengthen the local belief of ghosts. Inside scratched and peeling brown paint, varnish and scrumble hid delightful wood carvings and ancient oak panelling, whilst torn and dingy wallpaper hardly covered crumbling plaster. Despite the sad appearance of the property Captain Neil and Mrs Forsyth decided one hot June afternoon to buy Pashley and try to restore it to its original splendour.

During their fifteen-year occupation extensive work was carried out and much of the original structure and decor revealed, including small mullioned wing windows either side of the three bay windows and wattle and daub plastering with original pargetting.

Some believe that it was because of the arrival of the builders that the ghost was disturbed. Who the ghost is nobody seems to know, but Lindsay Forsyth when she was about nine years of age frequently saw the phantom of an 'old lady in a grey dress walking through a partition wall from one bedroom to another'. There was nothing horrific or scaring about the appearance of the spectre, in fact when her father decided to brick up a fireplace in the wall Lindsay protested very strongly. 'The old lady won't be able to visit me now', she said. Presumably it was the same phantom as that seen by Madge, but another ghostly lady adds further evidence for the existence of an earlier building on the site. She was seen late one afternoon by a sensitive friend and neighbour of the Forsyths standing on the island in the pond known as 'the moat' just looking down into the water. After a few seconds the apparition 'just faded away', but behind her the phantom outline of 'a really old building' had been seen. There can be no question that this appearance must relate to a completely different period to that of the phantom on the stairs.

In 1960 the Forsyths sold Pashley and moved to Kent. The new owners, Doctor and Mrs Bruce Cole, aimed at continuing the restoration work, more especially as Mrs Cole's grandmother was a descendant of the May family who had occupied the house some three hundred years earlier.

They were told of previous owners having seen the ghost of an old woman in grey who, on walking down the stairs, would glide straight through the wall opposite. She had also been seen on the terrace gliding towards one of the pools.

Mrs Cole told me that although she never actually witnessed the phantom she was often aware of a 'benign presence' in the hallway. The entire family were thrilled when on removing some old plaster from the wall facing the stairs the carved framework of a Tudor doorway was revealed, thus explaining why the 'little old lady' was 'melting into the wall'. She was walking through the original front door.

But these two ladies are not the only phantoms of Pashley.

Once when Rufus, one of Mrs Cole's eight children, was lying ill in a small room next to his mother's bedroom another apparition made its appearance.

The door to his nursery was ajar and kept slightly open by a sausage-shaped draught excluder on the floor. For the benefit of the children the light was kept on all night in the corridor and Mrs Cole's bedroom door was also wide open. One particular night she woke to see silhouetted in the doorway a small figure about four and a half feet tall clothed, she thought, in a dressing gown. Believing it to be her small son she called out, 'What is it, Rufus?' The figure moved away and so Mrs Cole jumped out of her bed and ran to the child's room to find the little boy lying spread-eagled on the bed in a high fever.

She had to push the door open causing a slight rattling sound from the 'sausage'. Rufus therefore had not left his bed, for no noise had been heard prior to the appearance of the silhouette and the door was practically closed. Was this phantom the same child that she would hear calling out from the direction of the moat? The pitiful cry of 'Maa...my' was frequently heard when Mrs Cole was in the old kitchen, usually on a Saturday morning. The voice was weird and 'creepy', echoing as it was through the trees and across the terrace.

Another haunted area was the flat occupied by the gardener and his wife at the end of the main building, accessible only by way of an outside stairway. Several times definite footsteps had been heard walking up the stairs though nobody was visible. When standing at the bottom of the stairs one evening the eldest son of the family had been scared by hearing the sounds pass him and walk on up to the flat. His mother felt, without being able to say why, that there was some evil influence connected with the phenomena.

Even the team of workmen were, it seems, affected by the atmosphere of the building for they flatly refused to be left alone and would depart whenever faced with the possibility.

Eventually the Coles had to move even though reluctant to do so, and sold the manor to a builder. But it seems that he was unable to carry out his original plans for the house and in 1972 sold it to the current owners Mrs and Mrs Le May, unrelated to the May family of earlier days.

David Le May told me that so far none of his family have ever seen any signs of the ghosts, but weird noises have often been heard in various parts of the building. 'There is always the chance', he said, 'that the old lady will appear some time'. His intention was, he told me, to complete the enormous job of restoring the manor before two years were out.

He showed me the huge inglenook fireplaces, one of which, in the main hall, is still being opened up to reveal a very large old fire-back. In another room timbers are being specially carved to replace those beyond repair. Paint was also being carefully removed to display the original texture and attractive graining of the ancient oak and the delicately moulded pine throughout the building.

Walking from room to room, dodging holes in the floors, but admiring here a magnificent Tudor fireplace with a fire-back decorated with the arms of the May family, there a shaped architrave or an early oak door, I could not help but wonder who the old lady was who regularly frequents the upper floor. The description hardly fits that of Ann Boleyn, but suggests an early Victorian lady. Would she, perhaps, be related to the Mays?

Once outside again I was filled with admiration at Mr Le May's confidence that the work would be completed within two years. I glanced upwards to see the barge board with the date 1621 put there by Anthony May to celebrate the finishing of the Tudor house, but it was too dark for me to see it.

We stood in the driveway for a few moments again admiring the attractive and picturesque frontage, hidden away as it is from the sight and sound of traffic on the main road. In fact, the only sound we heard was an owl adding an eerie touch to the surroundings.

Reluctantly driving away, I wondered whether the problem of identifying either of the two phantom ladies will ever be answered.

But one cannot help feeling it does not really matter for they are part of the atmosphere, the charm, the interest, the attractiveness of the manor. Without them Pashley would perhaps be just another country mansion. As it is, the house is one of secrets that will, no doubt, remain forever to intrigue and mystify the families who live there.

CHAPTER 12

PUTTENDEN MANOR, LINGFIELD

Set in unspoiled Surrey countryside and practically surrounded by the River Eden lies the lovingly restored, heavily-timbered manor house of Puttenden. It was originally built by Reginald Sondes as a hall house during the reign of Edward IV but, from manorial records of 1272, there appears to be the possibility that there was a much earlier building there at one time.

In 1593 Sir Thomas Sondes, grandson of the builder, left Puttenden to his brother Sir Michael Sondes and in 1676 Sir George Sondes became the Earl of Feversham who, by his first wife, had two sons. His second marriage to one of the Villiers family produced two daughters, the younger eventually marrying Lord Rockingham.

A popular legend about Puttenden is that the elder son of the earl, rather an egotistical conceited young man, very aware of his position as heir to the estates, intensely annoyed his younger brother by his condescending attitude. The strain finally proved too much and in a fit of uncontrolled rage and jealousy the older boy was brutally murdered by his brother when the family were in residence in Surrey which was not often. Their normal home was, and still is, at Lees Court in Kent.

The younger son died soon after the killing and in memory of her boys their mother planted a pair of weeping ash trees which, when they grew, intertwined their branches in a symbolic embrace. A belief is that Puttenden will be a happy house as long as the trees remain.

The legend, however, took some time to operate for all the major male descendants of Lord Rockingham died out and, although other titled families took control, the pattern continued. The eldest sons always died before attaining the family inheritance.

In 1753 the trustees of Lewis Watson, who had changed his name from the Honourable Lewis Monson, sold Puttenden to Abraham Adkins who eventually became sheriff of the county. His family lived in the manor until Samuel Whitby purchased it in 1897 with the estate of 962 acres.

Only four years later, during the South African war, Puttenden was once again up for sale. The conflict must have had a serious effect on the owner's capital for he was a brother of a former Speaker of the House of Commons and therefore deeply involved in the world of politics and finance.

It was lucky for Puttenden that the new owner was the Honourable Mark Napier MP for it was he who started the massive scheme to restore the house to its former glory, but he also took the opportunity of enlarging the property by adding the north wing, with such expertise that it is difficult to distinguish it from part of the original.

It was during a magnificent summer day when I arrived to meet the current owner and to learn about the haunting of Puttenden.

Mr Brian Thompson was happily sitting astride a large mowing machine cutting the huge lawn at the front of the house. Minutes later we were both lounging on the new mown grass beneath one of the ancient apple trees enjoying the sun and the glorious view of the house in front of us.

The Thompsons took over Puttenden in 1966 with the aim of completing the full restoration so ably initiated by the Napiers. What they did not know was that the house contained not only hundreds of relics and souvenirs of former occupiers going back roughly two hundred years but also the shades of owners who had lived and died there.

I learnt that when they moved in, the feeling inside the

house was of a 'brooding antipathy' and it was with a sense of apprehension that the Thompsons began to refurbish and redecorate the rooms.

Shortly after their arrival they were joined by an au pair girl from Ireland. She was allocated the Victorian bedroom which, with her help, was restored from 'an absolute shambles'.

It is one of the smallest rooms in the house but by the time the family had completed their work on it in 1969 it had become a warm, cosy haven complete with an old iron bedstead discovered in the attic. Because of the enormity of the work involved on the property one or two of the building team often used this tiny room to sleep in overnight and would frequently ask about the young children who woke them early in the morning.

At that time the Thompson's own children, a daughter and a young son, were sleeping in another of the rooms where the restoration work had been completed and because of the joint efforts of all the family both were so tired from their labours that they would be the last, not the first, to wake.

The workmen's comments, puzzling though they were, remained unanswered, but when the young Irish girl moved in and began also to enquire about the children who arose so early the Thompsons became a little concerned. With what may be considered as great diplomacy they have now allocated this room to children of friends and relatives when they come to stay.

Mrs Christine Bell of Reigate who visited Puttenden quite recently told me that when in the corridor outside the room she heard the sound of children's voices close to her and because of the feeling she expected a crowd of youngsters to burst forth from the room at any moment. She was astonished when, on entering, she found it empty and the children's squeals of delight were 'just fading into the atmosphere'.

A Mr Pratt of Caterham, who actually saw what he thought was a nursemaid in the room 'surrounded by a group of young children clustering round the old woman's skirts', is more than likely to have been one of the few living people to actually witness Mrs Napier with her beloved young friends.

A few paces from the Victorian Room lies the master bedroom also used by the builders as temporary overnight accommodation. This, one of the most important rooms in the house, was formerly occupied by Mrs Philip Napier and on several occasions the workmen complained of disturbed nights, though nothing tangible was ever recognisable as the cause except the sounds of footsteps and rustling silk.

When the Thompsons took over Puttenden this room resembled something from a Dickens story, having remained locked and untouched since the death of Mrs Napier in 1936. Now it merely reminds one of the happy family atmosphere which must have existed then and has been regenerated by the new owners. A corner cupboard, used by Mrs Napier to make perfume in, still stands in its original niche and her Regency four-poster bed acts as a further reminder of a former age now past but never forgotten. No museum piece this, but a corner of the house preserved as it used to be, though still in daily use.

One day when Moira Thompson was dusting she picked up a small trinket box to polish it and suddenly felt the presence of someone in the empty room with her. She looked around but saw nothing though was aware of a feeling of annoyance issuing from her unseen companion. She replaced the box and the sensation of unease just 'wafted away' confirming her belief that Mrs Napier was a little jealous of the intrusion of a stranger into her bedroom.

From what is known of the former lady of Puttenden she must have been an extremely strong-willed, rather dominant character in the household. A neighbour once described her as 'a bit of a dragon' but, despite her forceful ways and general commanding nature, Mrs Napier was greatly loved and highly respected. The devotion of her husband, Philip, is evident in his adoration of her bedroom as a holy shrine and, probably, the long illness he suffered after her death.

It is believed that hauntings are caused by major emotional upsets or traumas and one can easily accept that the daughter of Sir Charles Harvey must have created, albeit unconsciously and unintentionally, several situations where all was far from calm. Feeling no doubt that her position demanded complete and utter respect and loyalty, the elderly lady would often have caused upsets among the adults but, as with the majority of older people, she adored and was adored by the children, indeed all children.

Proof of the love she held for the youngsters are the portraits of her family which decorate the walls of the bedroom. Among these prints is one of Nigel Napier who was forced by death duties to sell the whole of the estate as it stood. Because of this the Thompsons were able to salvage many interesting and fascinating relics of the olden days and recreate the atmosphere which existed in many of the rooms.

Highlight of this restoration is the nursery which contains many of the original toys found in various stages of dilapidation all over the house. Now, carefully and tenderly repaired, they form a unique collection strengthening the overall pictures of childhood memories.

Elsewhere other reminders of the Napiers' occupation gaze down from walls or stare silently at visitors. A portrait of the Honourable Anne, Maid of Honour to Queen Victoria, shares the magnificent dining-room with a stag's head and the bust of the Honourable Mark, grandfather of Nigel Napier. Another more permanent sign of earlier owners can also be found in the same room for arms of the Sondes family are carved into the fireplace lintel and for further evidence of the founders one has only to look at the magnificent table reputedly as old as the house. Lords of the manor held courts at it and the supporting manorial rolls of Puttendenbury from 1745 are still in existence.

But to return to the current ghosts, it was interesting to learn that the formidable Mrs Philip Napier had not only been felt in her bedroom and the Victorian Room, but also seen, albeit rather infrequently, in other parts of the house. Her appearances are sometimes accompanied by a sweet smell of perfume, probably one of those she herself mixed in the corner cupboard. Mr Thompson assured me that the phantom does not restrict her activities to one locality for, on one occasion when entering his study, he felt a slight breeze and a gentle push as she passed by.

It is in the study that Philip Napier spent many solitary hours after the sad death of his wife. So distressed was the widower at his loss that his health deteriorated rapidly and the state of Puttenden declined. He could obviously see no further purpose in maintaining a property in which he had lost all interest. More than half his reason for living had gone and what remained was mere 'bricks and mortar'. His only enjoyment was to sit quietly in his study remembering the happy days, smoking a pipe and reclining in his favourite chair.

Even this old gentleman's presence remains for the smell of pipe tobacco frequently swirls round the walls of the room whilst Brian Thompson sits in the same chair in the same room and at the same desk dealing with the pile of correspondence and matters of business which the running of Puttenden demands.

So despite the wholesale restoration carried out by the Thompsons or perhaps more than likely because of it and their own homely family atmosphere the phantoms of Puttenden remain to form an integral part of the life of the manor. Mrs Napier continues to make her presence known as she must have done so many times in the past and also continues to mother her small charges. Those children unable still to leave the home that provided so much joy and happiness continue to play and share their pleasure with the nannie who cares for them with such kind and gentle devotion.

The old Mr Napier, though never seen, is also reluctant to depart from the place where he and his wife were so content.

Rather overshadowed by his wife's character it is not difficult to realise why he hardly ever makes his presence known. He must have 'taken the back seat' when alive and there is no reason why that situation should change now.

Having visited every room in the house, soaked up its charm and comfort, its warmth and friendliness, attributes identical to the entire Thompson family, I was reluctant to leave and return to the brash hard world outside. But leave I had to and as Mr Thompson bade me farewell I glanced back at the weeping ash trees clasped forever, it seems, in fond embrace. 'There is no doubt about it', I said, 'Puttenden is a happy house'. Brian smiled with pride. 'It's a *family* house', he said.

CHAPTER 13

GUILDFORD

The High Street of Guildford has been described as one of
of the finest streets in southern England, for its architecture
forms a remarkable blend of old and new. The height of
contrast varies from the clock dated 1683 fitted to the Guildhall and the Abbot's Hospital begun in 1619 to the new civic
centre and the thoughtful design of some recently constructed
shops. A more prominent comparison of the town could be
between the Norman Keep and the stark lines of the Surrey
University or the simple and modern cathedral which took
some thirty years to complete.

Exhibits in the museum housed in the castle arch give
some indication of the real age of Guildford, for here are
displayed items from the sixth-century Saxon cemetery and
pottery from an iron age dwelling site on the outskirts of the
town.

The arts are well represented by the Yvonne Arnaud
Theatre, ideally sited beside the old mill once operated by
the River Wey, and the former home of the Reverend Charles
Dodgson, better known as Lewis Carroll. The author of
Alice in Wonderland is believed to have told his tales to
young relatives in the surrounding countryside and many
souvenirs of his work are also retained in the museum. He
died in his family home at Guildford in 1898.

It is believed that the original name was Gilt Ford because
of the glorious golden buttercups carpeting the banks of the
Wey which flows through the valley at one end of the town.
There is no connection with Guilds for these were not even

thought of until many years after the foundation of the city.

For centuries Guildford has been a major home for devout worshippers. The number and variety of churches in the town and the completion of the prominent cathedral only a few years ago bears evidence of this. But it may not be realised that the Society of Friends chose the town as the site for one of their first homes.

In 1643 George Fox, a nineteen-year-old son of a Leicester weaver, felt he had received a divine call and as a result left home to wander about the country with bible in hand publicly expressing his disapproval of church bells, 'steeple houses' and many other accepted symbols of formal religion. A further 'revelation' experienced some three years later produced 'an inner light' in his heart and strengthened his convictions and attitudes towards the established church.

He frequently interrupted services when the preacher was teaching doctrines which he felt were erroneous and was imprisoned in Nottingham in 1649 for his behaviour. In the following year he was gaoled in Derby on a charge of blasphemy and on his release walked barefoot through Lichfield cursing the town.

Despite numerous further prison sentences he was persuasive enough to gather a group of dedicated followers to him and in 1656 nearly a thousand of his supporters were in gaol. The group insisted on interpreting Christ's words literally, thus opposing war and the taking of oaths, yet promoting poor relief and self help. Their form of speech with their 'thees' and 'thous' to all regardless of station, position or wealth, both annoyed and amused the general populace. To Fox, the Sacrament and Baptism were unnecessary and there was no need at all for ordained or paid officials.

Gaining financial support from all levels, the rich providing insurance for themselves and the poor aiming at helping others, he was able to visit Jamaica and America in 1671 and Holland in 1677 and 1684 'spreading the word' and obtaining more followers. Early Quakers 'shaking with the power of the

Holy Ghost' would often express their feelings towards convention by walking naked through the streets.

The term 'Quakers' had already been given to the Sect in 1650 by Mr Justice Gervase Bennet having been admonished by the founder to 'tremble at the word of the Lord' and it was about this time that the first meeting house was opened in London. About twenty years later the Children of Light, Friends of Truth or the Society of Friends, their own titles for the group, purchased a building on the south side of North Street, Guildford, and a plot of land opposite as a burial ground.

One of the first local families to join the 'new religion' lived in Sydenham Road, practically next door to where the Holy Trinity Church stands. They were ardent and devoted in their support of the movement and attempted with considerable enthusiasm to indoctrinate all their friends and relatives in the society's principles and beliefs. Lorna, their daughter, was disinterested and unconvinced and preferred to occupy her spare time with her boy-friend.

The question of religion between these two never arose. They had other things to do and think about than 'life hereafter'. The father, intense and intolerant as ever, would continually question Lorna about her boy-friend. How old was he? What were his parents like? What was his attitude towards religion? This constant pestering caused the usual result inasmuch as Lorna, bordering on twenty years of age, grew away from her parents, became sullen and dispirited calling on solace only from her lover. She was an attractive teenager, tall, slim with light auburn hair and grey-blue eyes and had a mind of her own. They would be married some time, so what did it matter?

One fateful evening nearing Christmastime her father discovered the couple together and demanded to know of the boy what faith he supported. The answer was far from satisfactory and the older man in a rage threatened to throw Lorna into the street there and then. Unconventionality was all right for the society but not for the unconverted. His daughter would marry only a devoted 'friend' and not any Tom, Dick or Harry. How dare a lad who should know better consort with Lorna without realising she was a Quaker. He had not even asked to join the élite set.

It is a good thing that this fanatic was not typical of the movement which, in 1947, won the Nobel Prize for international reconciliation.

Lorna, appalled at the sight of her storming father and his irrational attitude, attempted to reason with him. Lorna's boy-friend, embarrassed by the family quarrel, slipped away.

The row grew more intense, more heated, more illogical. The girl, incensed by her parent's behaviour, had reached her limit. 'All right, Father. You want me out of the house. I'll leave now', and grabbing a small black cap she ran out still wearing her long grey evening gown.

Understandably not knowing her destination, she ran down to the main street, crossed it and continued on to the old chalk pits. Unheeding of the brambles which tore her legs, her arms, her dress, she ran on in her fury, then, suddenly reaching a crumbling edge of a small quarry, tripped and fell headlong into a quagmire of sodden chalk.

It was quite some time before she was discovered suffering from severe exposure, torn flesh, multiple bruises and several broken bones. She was carried back to her home but it was too late. She died shortly afterwards.

Her father, still outraged at her behaviour, refused to forgive his daughter despite heartfelt entreaties from his sorrowing wife and even pleas from other members of the society. Neither his beliefs nor his principles would be shaken. The girl's body would not be buried in the family grave. Anywhere else, but not with 'friends' in the Quakers' Acre.

This small plot of land, unused for many years, was presented to the town some fifty years ago and now forms a pleasant public garden behind the old Abbot's Hospital.

In the 1960s, because of its popularity as an ideal shopping and attractive tourist centre, Guildford realised that drastic action should be taken to provide more extensive car parking facilities.

The only site was that in Sydenham Road and, after several compulsory purchases and demolitions, a new multi-storey structure began to take shape. By 1969 finishing touches were hurriedly being made to the barriers on the second floor in order to get the facilities ready in time for the Christmas rush of traffic.

Two of the workmen painting the wooden fencing suddenly noticed the figure of a woman standing silently at the edge of the floor. One of the men called out and started to walk towards the trespasser. She turned to face him and he stopped, struck by her beauty. 'It was a girl. Thin face with sort of grey-blue eyes and golden brown hair, but she looked terribly sad. I remember though that the colour of her dress seemed to match her eyes'.

Just as the man was about to enquire as to whether he could help, the figure slowly vanished, just 'faded away like a mist!' The spot at which the phantom was seen would probably have been that of her bedroom, the site of that last terrible row with her father and the room where, after trying to escape, she returned to die. A pitiful tale, but perhaps one with a moral calling for more religious tolerance.

Only a few days later, remains of a very old well were found below the foundations of an adjoining property which had to be demolished.

A more puzzling story concerns the *Angel Hotel,* the town's oldest inn near the bottom of the High Street. I have often enjoyed a superb meal here and, like so many customers and the staff, am still mystified by the incident which occurred early one morning in January 1970.

Mr and Mrs Dell were staying a couple of nights in the Prince Imperial of France Room, so named because of the belief that this illustrious 'royal' was once a guest here. The couple prepared for bed after a visit from some friends and Mr Dell was sitting facing a large mirror fitted to the door of a large wardrobe. Suddenly, whilst chatting to his wife, he saw a figure appear in the glass and he glanced round. The room was empty except for his wife sitting on the edge of the bed.

Mr Dell quickly found the only piece of paper available, a red serviette, and made a sketch of the figure with his ball point pen. Mrs Dell was unable to see the apparition at first, but within a few seconds realised that she too was looking at a phantom. A photograph of the sketch appeared later in the local paper, *The Surrey Advertiser,* and from the details provided it was established that the spectre was of a Polish soldier in a late nineteenth-century uniform. Why he visited the *Angel* nobody has been able to establish, though there have been hints of a fatal duel fought in the hotel in the last century and a suggestion that he might have been connected with the Franco-Prussian War, without any reason being offered.

What may be a clue to the incident was the old bullet found in one of the oak beams by Mr Madden of the Surrey Trust during some renovation work on the ground floor.

The only other phenomena experienced in No 1 bedroom was that in November 1969 when a lady guest contacted the reception desk at 8pm to report that there was an 'unseen presence in the room' and requested that she be moved to another room. The clerk went to find out what was wrong and discovered the guest standing alone in the room shivering with fright.

Seemingly unconnected with these incidents at the *Angel* is the thirteenth-century vaulted crypt used as a restaurant, but believed to be of monastic origin and which, according to legend, was linked through an old tunnel to the castle a few hundred yards away.

Despite its size and its age, Guildford itself has very few phantoms of the past and with these two exceptions no other hauntings have ever been recorded though rumours were rife in the eighteenth century that the ancient hospital, now an old folks' home, was visited somewhat infrequently by a former member of the medical profession.

On the other side of the High Street the boys' school founded by Henry VIII, should perhaps be another candidate for the classification of being haunted, for early this century a young pupil became terribly worried at seeing one of his father's grooms enter an empty classroom and vanish. The following day the lad received a note telling him that as a result of an accident involving a coach one of the grooms had been killed. This turned out to be at precisely the same time as his spectre was seen eight miles away in the school.

I used to live in Linersh Wood Close, Bramley, some four miles south of Guildford on the Cranleigh road. As the name implies, before the development of the estate it was a large, privately-owned wood which only started to be opened up just before the second world war. Remains of the old canal connecting the Wey Navigation with the Portsmouth and Arundel canal can still be found in some of the front gardens in the long cul-de-sac.

There is a narrow twisting country road leading from Shalford to Bramley and, near the junction with the Wonersh road, several evening travellers have been surprised to see an old gypsy woman leading a decrepit brown horse down towards Wonersh.

The area was a favourite one for Romany encampments and there used to be a large group temporarily accommodated in the woods. The attraction was the seclusion, the close proximity of Cranleigh Waters and the possibility of occasional but profitable contact with the bargees.

One of the most recent witnesses to the appearance of the gypsy was a chief pilot of the British European Airways. He had collected his young daughter from dancing lessons in Shalford and slowing down as he drew near the figures turned to the girl and said, 'I wonder where they are going'.

His daughter, obviously puzzled by the comment, pointed out that 'it was only an old horse, Daddy'. The pilot, astonished, realised that the old woman was invisible to his daughter and was even more shocked when a few yards further on both apparitions vanished.

Some years ago, when exploring the stream at the bottom of my garden, I discovered stone foundations of an ancient bridge later confirmed as medieval and a couple of relics suggesting that the wooden bridge had collapsed whilst someone on a horse had been on it.

Later I learnt that the new owners of the garden had found more human and animal remains on the stream bed, consisting of a pair of very old leather sandals and several bones of a horse. Had some tragedy occurred there which was connected in some way with the gypsy bringing a replacement horse to the site?

In Bramley High Street, snuggling against the bridge over a stream, there is an old timbered building hanging over the narrow strip of clear, moving water. It was built late in the seventeenth century, and about a hundred years ago housed a young lady who suffered the desertion of her lover. So intense was her affection for him that, unable to live any longer with her broken heart, she had committed suicide.

One evening, at the time her boy-friend would usually arrive, she had stood in the doorway for some minutes as she had so many times before and then, with a heart-rending cry, ran upstairs to her bedroom and flung herself out of the window into the water.

Her thin white figure has sometimes been seen standing pitifully inside the shop just in front of where a door was blocked up in the nineteenth century. 'She just stands there like a little white shadow until she fades away back into her own time'.

The adjoining village of Wonersh consists mainly of groups of ancient cottages, some of them formerly stables of a manor house demolished in the 1800s, the *Grantley Arms,* a seventeenth-century inn, and the church of St John the Baptist, parts of which were constructed in the eleventh century.

There are two oddities in the church. One of these is a marble tomb with imprints of brass shields on the sides. Each autumn the tomb weeps cassia, the liquid in which the remains were embalmed over three hundred years ago. Despite several attempts to seal the cracks through which the brown sticky fluid seeps it continues its annual performance.

The other peculiarity is the little chamber or crypt hidden by the altar. Several suggestions have been made for its original use, the most popular being that it formed a charnel house or contained holy relics.

A few hundred yards away off the village High Street are situated a small cluster of mews flats, survivors of the many stables. In the 1950s a professor of zoology moved into one of these flats to use as a study for he intended to carry out a programme of intense research into a particular problem.

He worked satisfactorily for some weeks, but in quiet moments of concentrated thought he realised that there was some peculiar atmosphere in the small room. A silent, rather forbidding, presence seemed to lurk in one corner. A half shadow which never moved, sombre and powerful. The scientist tried to ignore its growing intensity. He tried vainly to shut his mind to the power which seemed to be gradually affecting his thoughts. He tried to ignore the dark movements of the shadow seen only at the edges of his eyesight.

One evening, realising that his work was being affected, he spent nearly half an hour examining the room, concentrating on the far corner for some logical explanation of the phenomena. There was nothing to be found, nothing to be seen which would account for the ever present gloom or the sense of icy fear he felt when nearing that particular wall.

He tried to speed up his work, but found only that his mind more frequently wandered to what it was that cowered threateningly in the room. No longer could he concentrate, but was reluctant to leave, reluctant and shamed to admit defeat to the invisible power of unutterable evil, a force which insinuated thoughts of death into his mind.

Getting more and more despondent he realised that unless he took some definite action his life would be in danger. 'The feeling was diabolical. I was developing suicidal tendencies. I was even considering various ways by which I could kill myself. I just had to get out before it was too late'.

But it was a race that the professor thankfully won. He quickly found a new home in Bramley and moved in but, he assured me, 'it was a close thing. I am convinced that if I had remained there for more than a couple of days I would have killed myself'.

What was, or is, that nameless horror which haunts and pervades that tiny establishment? There is only a rumour which can be offered as a possible answer. Some years previously an artist in a studio somewhere in Wonersh is known to have committed suicide by drinking a poison he concocted himself, some say from local weeds, others from chemicals. There is even one tale which implies he was dabbling in black magic which 'went wrong'. Whether the site is that of the professor's weird experience is not known and is now a matter of conjecture. A rather disturbing one.

CHAPTER 14

CATERHAM AND KENLEY

It is widely known that past incidents in a property are sometimes likely to affect existing occupiers. In a house in Montpelier Road, Ealing, no less than twenty suicides and a murder were recorded before the building was pulled down in the 1970s. In this particular case one could ponder on the thought that even the road itself is affected for at one end a hotel was claimed to be haunted by three ghosts and in the building opposite 'The House of Suicides' a murder occurred in 1954 which achieved national interest.

John Donald Merrett, calling himself Ronald Chesney, in attempting to steal his wife's money found it necessary to drown her in a bath. Disturbed by his mother-in-law, Mrs Bonner, known as 'Lady Menzies', he realised he must murder her also. One result of this double crime was that some twenty-eight old 'gentlewomen' housed by Lady Menzies at No 22 for some years had to be provided with new homes by the Greater London Council and in 1973 the house was reported as haunted by 'mysterious screams and moans near the bottom of the stairs', the site of the second killing.

Chesney, having escaped the police net, shot himself in a wood near Cologne on 16 February 1954, five days after becoming a famous criminal. He had by then confessed to killing his mother in Scotland when only seventeen years of age.

Could it be that Welcomes Road and the adjoining Hayes Lane, Kenley, also have some peculiar atmosphere which once affected the area?

Early in 1920 the Reverend Gordon Tombe called upon

Superintendent Francis Carlin of Scotland Yard to advise him of the concern the priest had for Eric, his son. His wife had constantly dreamt that Eric was dead and had 'seen' his body lying at the bottom of a well, believed to be in the grounds of a stud farm in Hayes Lane, Kenley.

The priest's son, George Eric Tombe, had met another enthusiastic horse lover and together they raised five thousand pounds and bought Welcomes Farm with the intention of training and breeding horses. The plan could have been successful even though Eric had little real knowledge of the business but Ernest Dyer, his partner, took only a few weeks before admitting his real interest was in racing cars and not horses.

Unknown to Eric, the farm had been insured by Dyer for twelve thousand pounds, but whilst Eric was away in the north of England a major fire burnt down a considerable portion of the property and the insurance company refused to pay the claim.

A year later the partnership was dissolved and neither of the men had been heard of since.

In March 1920, shortly after the visit of the Reverend Tombe, the police began to make enquiries and various unsavoury incidents regarding Dyer's activities were disclosed. Partly through forgery the partner had been able to steal nearly £3,000 from the farm's account. The search for the criminal was intensified and in July of the same year a man calling himself Fitzsimmons thought to be passing 'dud' cheques was shot dead in a struggle with the local police in a hotel in Scarborough.

Among his personal articles were 180 blank cheques signed in pencil by an 'Eric Tombe' and other evidence proving that Fitzsimmons was Ernest Dyer.

The police then switched their interest to Welcomes Farm. By now it was a desolate ruin with grounds waist high in brambles and shrubs and the wreck of the home itself practically hidden beneath weeds.

Diligent searching revealed the existence of five wells and, by the time the police had partially cleared the area and investigated two of them without success, night had fallen.

Lamps were called for and work commenced on the third well. Shortly after midnight the remains of what proved to be the body of Eric Tombe were recovered. He had been shot in the back of the head.

Evidence gained from Dyer's widow and a girl-friend, although officially 'circumstantial', proved beyond doubt that Tombe had been murdered by his partner some time during the evening of Mrs Tombe's first dream of her son.

Some forty years later in the summer of 1966 a group from the local archaeological society carried out a 'dig' in an attempt to discover the exact location of the medieval village of Wattendone before the development of a new housing estate hid it for another few hundred years. Locals immediately recalled the last time a similar search was carried out, for the present Waddington abuts Kenley, and is only a few yards from Welcomes Farm and Welcomes Road.

First mention of the village was in the ninth century but, at the time of the Domesday Book, the Abbey of St Peter of Chersey 'held' Watendone which, with its church, was worth six pounds. This church, described as a chapel, was granted to a William Ward during the reign of Edward VI and used as a barn until about 1780 when a fire destroyed all but the walls which were still standing in 1808.

Numerous clues as to the location of the village provided considerable assistance to the archaeologists. A bend in Hayes Lane suggested the road was curved to avoid a settlement, or, as some suggest, 'a village deserted because of the Black Death', and, in 1900 when Watendone Manor was being constructed, human bones were discovered. Confirmation of the location resulted from the excavations in 1966, for about twenty skeletons of a christian-type burial and foundations of a building strongly believed to be those of the original church were revealed. Watendone had been rediscovered, but whilst the diggers were hard at work numerous enquiries were made by interested visitors as to whether they were looking for 'The Grey Lady of Kenley'.

This ghostly female is that of a nun frequently seen up to a few years ago in the immediate locality. Efforts to establish her history have proved fruitless, though locals have associated the name 'Sister Mary' with the apparition.

One evening shortly after the end of the war a tenant of Welcomes Cottages in Hayes Lane, a few yards from the chapel site, was awoken from a doze by hearing her baby scream. She ran downstairs and on bursting into the bedroom was shocked to see a misty shape in the form of a woman bending over her child's cot. As the mother ran to comfort the youngster the ghost just faded away.

It was not long before another report concerning the Grey Lady visiting the area was made. An Indian ayah chatting to her employer in Welcomes Road said that she was very reluctant to walk along the road in the evenings because of the 'lady in dirty white who was not of this world'. To an Indian nanny the repeated appearance of the phantom wearing anything but pure white was strange anyway.

In a house in Welcomes Road, claimed to be on the site of an old 'monks' walk', the delightful perfume of narcissus used to waft through one of the rooms. Not only were the owners aware of this peculiar phenomena but numerous visitors would comment on the 'lovely scent' and would be puzzled when it changed to that of candle grease. In the same house, built in the 1880s, footsteps were frequently heard in the evening walking straight through the house.

Mrs Howland, then owner of Welcomes Farm, happened one day to glance towards Barn Cottages in Hayes Lane and saw the figure of a lady in a grey gown in the front garden. Mistaking it for Mrs Fretwell, mother of the owner of the cottages, she waved and called out a greeting. Only when the shape faded away did Mrs Howland realise that she had been another witness of 'Sister Mary'.

The appearance of the nun has been so frequent to so many people and at such varying times that there can be no doubt as to her authenticity. An example of the ghost's daytime wandering was when a gentleman driving home from work one afternoon in 1968 was puzzled at seeing 'what looked like a nun walking in my driveway'. Because she seemed to be deaf to his horn and the sound of his car he stopped and got out to ask the lady to move so that he could continue his journey down the narrow lane leading to his house. But as he neared the figure it just melted into the hedgerow.

In Barn Cottages Mrs Fretwell senior saw the Sister beneath a magnificent cedar tree in the back garden and some years later her bereaved husband also saw the spectral nun in the same spot. A maid living in the same house had twice mistaken the apparition for her employer's mother. The younger Mr Fretwell when working in a shed adjoining the cottage was surprised one evening to see the figure glide past him into the garden making its way, one supposes, to the cedar tree. To add further to the programme of the nun's appearances she was seen three times at 8 o'clock in the morning in the hall of one of the cottages.

Who was Sister Mary? What is the significance of that glorious cedar?

It has not been unknown for the phantom nun on a few occasions to be seen carrying a pitiful bundle resembling a baby and the cottages now known as 'Barn Cottages' and 'Brambles' were believed to have been built on a monastery on the outskirts of the ancient village of Watendone. Some years ago during the demolition of Garston Hall near Old Lodge Lane, another road leading off Hayes Lane, the remains of an old tunnel leading towards the cottages was discovered which strengthened local belief that the Hall covered foundations of a convent which was linked to the home of a group of monks.

A picture begins to emerge.

One can easily imagine Sister Mary having fallen passionately in love with a member of the brotherhood making secret trysts with him beneath the cedar tree in a quiet peaceful corner of the village. There they would talk of their mutual love and affection. The man, no doubt, worried a little with his conscience, beliefs and vows would perhaps have been a little more reticent than his adoring companion in revealing emotions. But there, beneath the sheltering branches, perhaps sitting on the wall of an old rainwater well holding hands like any lovers, the couple would talk, happy in each other's company though concerned with their future.

I have walked Hayes Lane many times but less frequently down Welcomes Road which has its own aura of peacefulness and individuality. Guarded and partially hidden by the trees of Kenley Common it is an ideal spot for those wishing to enjoy a semi-rural atmosphere within a stone's throw of the suburban Purley and the bustling cluster of shops at Caterham.

Looking through the dense undergrowth of Kenley Common, with its thickly grouped trees swaying gently in an evening breeze, one hardly needs any imagination to picture the solitary figure of Sister Mary, clutching the small bundle that was once pitiful evidence of a few passionate moments.

Whilst in those dark, sometimes sombre woods local children used to play round a small cave or 'grotto' which used to be associated with the haunting. Rumour has it that it was a personal altar used by the nun for private prayer and confession, others are more morbid and suggest it was a tomb of a child, though nothing was ever found to suggest this.

Conjecture is called for when trying to find a reason for the nun's travels. Some, those who have witnessed the woman alone, feel she is looking for that tiny bundle of life which they think was murdered by the father. Others who have seen Sister Mary gently carrying the child in her arms believe she searches for her lover who, it seems, brutally left her.

But the picture may of course be more sorrowful. The priest could have been the victim of the Black Death or of his own religious order who could have punished the erring brother with banishment to another monastery or even worse. Yet another possibility is that the baby itself fell victim to the plague and the overwrought mother, unable to be parted from her child, continues to carry the pitiful armful.

Whatever caused the haunting will remain unknown, for it seems that with the revealing of the lost medieval village site Sister Mary has practically ceased her phantom travels. What was there among the pile of human bones which were a mere thirty feet from the chapel? On the edge of the burial ground a mysterious pile of charcoal was found and, in the centre of the rectangular foundations at one end of the thirteenth-century chapel, traces of a probable earlier building were discovered. Were either of these connected with the death of a child and the disappearance of the monk?

Maybe one day an enthusiastic gardener digging his plot will be puzzled to find some small object which will add a further clue to the haunting by Sister Mary.

At 10.30am one Saturday in the same year as the 'dig' by the Bourne Society a Mr Ginsbury in a flat in Westway, Caterham on the Hill, about a mile from the nun's walk, suddenly heard the door to his flat slam shut and footsteps running down the stairway. He was puzzled, for he thought he was alone in the building except for his teenage sister studying in the next room. Going to find the cause of the disturbing noise he realised that there was no answer to the problem. He and his sister were alone.

The inexplicable sounds were repeated at the same time every Saturday for the following three weeks but by then the unseen visitor had caused several knockings and tappings on the inside of the front door to be heard not just by him but also by his father and sister. Mr Ginsbury senior also heard something knocking on the wall immediately behind his bed.

The only information they were able to obtain was that the

previous tenant of the flat had been extremely unhappy there and is thought to have committed suicide.

Another half mile to the south east, leading away from the roundabout at Caterham, is Godstone Road, the old route to Godstone before the construction of the A22 bypassed Caterham. Some of the houses on one side of the road were built in 1859 on a field named *Scaldshill*. At that time these multi-storeyed semi-detached properties were the latest fashion for well-to-do Victorians desirous of moving into the newly-developed area of Caterham which had by then gained a certain amount of popularity because of the introduction of the railway to the area.

About 1880 one of these houses was sold to a Mrs Betty Sharpe who decided to retain the name of the house *Scaldshill* despite the fact that the field was no longer in existence. It merely formed part of her back garden but she also joined her neighbours by numbering her new home. It became number 108.

Betty spent an uneventful life in the house, dying at the age of ninety-six in March 1957. The new owners, Mr Eddie Pratt and his wife Johanna, moved in and arranged for some close friends to rent the top flat.

A couple of weeks later whilst pelmets were still being fitted, carpets laid and the general bustle of settling in was under way, Eddie in the hallway happened to glance up the stairway to his friend's flat and was surprised to see an old lady wearing a lace shawl and a long dark Victorian gown standing on the landing looking down at him. Wondering who the old visitor was, he smiled and called out 'hello'. With that the figure slowly vanished and 'just melted away'.

Mr Pratt felt it unwise to mention the incident to his wife so was slightly amused when a few weeks later Johanna asked him if he had seen 'the funny little old woman on the landing'. Neither of the couple were at all frightened by the ghost's appearance, merely assuming that they had received a visit from the past. There are not many people who would fail to be curious at the activities of new occupiers to what had been their home for well over seventy years.

Shortly after they had settled in, Eddie's sister asked whether her young daughter could stay with them for a holiday and the event became a regular annual one. The visits of the old Mrs Sharpe however became less frequent, but naturally no mention of her appearance was ever made to guests.

One day in 1962, however, the twelve-year-old niece, having returned for a day trip after staying with the Pratts for a few weeks earlier in the year, suddenly asked her uncle 'who is the little old lady on the stairs?'

Not only is Betty Sharpe visible to the owners, but to at least one young visitor who is as unconcerned as the Pratts at the curiosity of such a 'pleasant and friendly old soul. After all, she adds to the companionship of the place'.

CHAPTER 15

THE CROWN INN, OXTED

There are hundreds of haunted pubs in England although many of the stories surrounding them are, I feel, the products of imagination, a desire for publicity or just too much elbow-raising. There was, for instance, an alleged haunting in a Midlands pub involving a pair of phantoms having a sword fight in the saloon bar, but this unusual occurrence was only reported when the monthly takings were down and on enquiry I was assured that the only person who had seen the ghostly battle was the licensee himself. Unfortunately for the believers of the story the publican involved died a few years ago in a mental hospital.

Despite this sort of incident there are many genuine haunt-ings in licensed establishments. There are basically three types of hostelries in this country; those that were originally linked with churches offering sustenance and refreshment to pilgrims, others that were built as private houses or shops and have become pubs because of the ideal siting of the building or owing to local demand, and the balance, the modern variety, that were actually built as public houses.

One in the second category is *The Crown* in Oxted. The western section of the original building was probably con-structed some time in the eighteenth century as a house or shop facing on to the main street. It is known that one area, now the dining-room, was once used for the storage of hay which could suggest that the building might have been a forge. In the middle of the 1800s an additional wing was added on the eastern side, but by then it had already become a popular inn. In recent years an old wooden settle was found in what had been the storeroom implying that *The Crown* has been a pub for at least a hundred years, possibly much longer. A painting by R. H. Yates in the local library gives some idea of the appearance of the pub in the 1870s.

In the mid-1930s the licensee was a Charlotte La Mont whose husband, a French Canadian, was far from the ideal. Very little is known of the early days of the couple, but Charlotte, a pleasant cheerful soul, was highly respected: after all, she was English. Her husband, it seems, was a lazy drunkard unable to understand her attitudes, her efficiency or much of her language. Mrs La Mont, always polite and lively with her customers, was a conscientious woman, seeing to it that the accounts balanced and orders were fulfilled as speedily as possible.

There is no question about who wore the trousers in the house. Realising the character of her ne'er-do-well companion, Charlotte was forced to take more command and more control of the business. She was a woman in a man's world and therefore took the running of the pub much more seriously than a man might have done.

Her husband could not be ignored of course. He was vital when it came to the cellar work, and the odd occasion when an awkward customer refused to depart quietly. Slowly, however, the relationship between the two worsened.

For the next couple of years Pierre, the husband, realising that he was merely degenerating into a 'hired help' consumed more and more alcohol. And not only was he drinking away the profits, but added to the worsening position by liberally giving his special cronies free drinks. There is always someone who takes advantage of such a situation and *The Crown* seemed to have its fair share of such 'freebooters'.

The reputation of the pub was seriously affected. Constant rows and visits from the police and the brewers did not pass unnoticed by the more respectable characters. Fewer of them came for their evening 'constitutional' and the profits dwindled.

Charlotte tried vainly to ignore the half-empty bars, the lack of regular quality customers and the severe reduction in the monthly takings. When upstairs, working on the books or carrying out the normal household chores, she had often heard Pierre shouting 'Drinks all round' in an effort, it seemed, to buy friendship and to endear himself to the worthless topers of the village.

One evening, having finally decided it had to stop, the lady of the house called Pierre to her bedroom. They had not shared the same room for years, the drunkard habitually sleeping wherever he fell.

'Go!' she said. 'Go back to Canada. Get out!' Pleadings and threats were of no avail. Charlotte was determined. She could take the appalling situation no longer. She held the licence and was fully entitled to dispense with anyone who would affect her reputation and that of the pub. There was a position to uphold.

Pierre raged and shouted, begged and argued. It was no use. Still befuddled from constant drinking, he stormed out of the pub. He reached his homeland some months later, and disappeared into an instant obscurity.

Charlotte, freed from her unfortunate liability, attempted to rejuvenate *The Crown*. Her brother joined her and helped as much as he could, but he was unused to the licensed trade and proved little assistance.

It was August 1939; war clouds were brewing. In the pub, the couple seriously evaluated their future. There seemed to be two alternatives: either remain and try to re-establish the trade and reputation of the pub or leave the country. The man had friends and a job in South Africa and would be only too willing for his 'little sister' to come with him. They had no real friends in England. The answer was obvious and they took it.

Only a few months after the departure of Pierre, Mrs La Mont and her brother left the shores of Britain to start a new life in Capetown.

The war came and the new licensees found it difficult at first to build up trade. Slowly, however, figures improved and began to recover. New faces and new residents brought a more cheerful atmosphere into *The Crown* and the 'regulars' returned.

By 1960 the tenancy of the La Monts was practically forgotten, but an unusual incident experienced by Dennis Cornish, one of the barmen at the time of Bob Griffith's residence, brought back memories.

Occasionally tourists and commercial travellers would be provided with overnight accommodation in the pub, and one evening Dennis went upstairs to take a drink to a visitor in one of the rooms. As he reached the bend in the stairs he was astonished to see the clear outline of a woman standing on the landing. She was 'sort of half transparent and wearing the sort of dress women wore before the war, rather long'.

The barman blinked and the figure just 'slowly faded away'. Dennis returned to the bar visibly shaken and Charlotte was never seen again, but she certainly made her presence felt.

Bob Griffiths claimed that on one occasion he and a group of customers were discussing Mrs La Mont when a lamp bulb over the bar 'just fell out. It had been up there for over a year. But what really was peculiar was about a week later exactly the same thing happened again'.

The most inexplicable phenomena, however, was the icy cold feeling in what had been Charlotte's bedroom. Many of the overnight travellers had complained of the cold in the room, whatever the temperature was outside, and despite numerous efforts to discover the cause the room remained bitterly cold.

The new licensee, John Lardner, was inclined to dismiss the sensation as 'imagination' and put an oil heater in the room for two weeks, but this made no difference to the temperature.

In August 1973, with two friends, I visited the bare empty room and was surprised by the intense cold of the atmosphere.

The room contained but one piece of furniture, an old wardrobe which looked as if it had not been moved since the days of Mrs La Mont. The only window, a grubby one, faced out on to the small courtyard at the side of the building and the end wall is an internal one for behind it is an old lean-to barn.

Never have I been in a room as icy as that in *The Crown*. Our breath issued from our mouths in steamy puffs as if we were standing in a refrigerated store.

At the time of our visit none of us knew the full story connected with the room, but were merely trying to find some logical explanation for the freezing atmosphere. Beneath us lay the bottle store, not warm by any means, but not nearly as cold as that bedroom.

Eddie, the more sensitive of the trio, suddenly went quiet and told us that he could see the figure of a middle-aged lady standing beside a bed. 'She is terribly angry,' he told us, 'and I get the feeling that the trouble is connected with her husband.' He continued giving a description of the phantom and later we found that it matched that given by Dennis Cornish.

Months afterwards we heard that for some unknown reason the temperature in that bedroom had suddenly become normal and the room is now happily used by overnight guests. However, several visitors have enquired about the intense feeling of cold at the top of the stairs, the spot where Charlotte must have stood, full of emotion, whilst she watched her drunken husband stumble out of her life.

One interested local went so far as to suggest that Charlotte pushed Pierre down the stairs to his death, hid the body somewhere and let it be known that he had returned to Canada. But no evidence of this has ever been found during the extensive renovations and modifications that have been carried out to the building. The only souvenirs of Pierre have been the numerous empty bottles discovered in various nooks and crannies, under floor boards, in dark cupboards and even in a chimney.

Another unconfirmed rumour connected with the French Canadian was that he was having an affair with a young woman from some nearby cottages. Is it coincidence that a phantom of an old man, thought to be that of the father, has recently been reported being seen standing in front of a fire-place in one of the adjoining houses?

What is a little unusual about this haunting is that foot-steps are also heard walking up the stairs and continuing beyond the existing stairway and into the cottage next door. I was unable to establish whether the building was originally one house at the time of Pierre's occupation in the nearby pub, but this would be the most obvious answer to the problem.

But there is no problem now in *The Crown*. The new licensees, for John Lardner left in December 1974, are con-vinced that Charlotte's experience and the rather frightening atmosphere she created on that traumatic night has at last dispersed, or at least moved to a less disturbing area of the building. I hope they are right.

BIBLIOGRAPHY

Archer, Fred. *Ghost Detectives* (1970)

Behrens, Mrs. *Under Thirty Kings* (1920)

Bourne Society's Local History Records Book VI (1967)

Butler, Ivan. *Murderer's London* (1973)

Fleming, Lindsay. *History of Pagham in Sussex* (1949)

Green, Andrew.

> *Our Haunted Kingdom* (1974)
>
> *Mysteries of Surrey* (1972)
>
> *Mysteries of Sussex* (1973)
>
> *Mysteries of London* (1973)
>
> *Ghost Hunting, A Practical Guide* (1973)
>
> *Haunted Houses* (1975)

Hallam, Jack. *Haunted Inns of England* (1972)

Mee, Arthur. *The King's England: Kent* (1936)

Owen, A. R. George, and Sims, Victor. *Science and The Spook* (1971)

Parkinson, C. Northcote. *Life and Times of Horatio Hornblower* (1973)

Pears, Molly. *Michelham Priory* (1970)

Strickland, Agnes. *Lives of the Queens of England* (1954)

Sussex County Magazine Vol 4 (1930)

Wood, Mrs Henry. *Argosy* (1880)